ALL ABOUT SPELLING

The Multisensory Program for Spelling Success

LEVEL three

by
MARIE RIPPEL

Contents

1 Preparing for Level Three

Gather the Materials 3

Set Up the Spelling Review Box 4

Organize the Letter Tiles 5

Take a Look at the Six Syllable Types 6

Review the Procedure for Spelling with Tiles 7

Learn How to Handle Troublemakers 8

Meet the New Teaching Tools 9

2 Complete Step-by-Step Lesson Plans

Step 1: Warming Up 13

Step 2: Vowel Teams AI and AY 19

Step 3: Ways to Spell /ā/ 23

Step 4: Silent E Book 27

Step 5: C+le Syllable Type, Part 1 31

Step 6: C+le Syllable Type, Part 2 35

Step 7: The /er/ of *Nurse* 41

Step 8: Y Can Say /ē/ 45

Step 9: Vowel Teams OA and OW 51

Step 10: Ways to Spell /ō/ 55

Step 11: Consonant Suffixes 59

Step 12: Vowel Suffixes 65

Step 13: The 1-1-1 Rule 69

Step 14: Words Beginning with WH 75

Step 15: The Sound of /o͞o/ Spelled OO 81

Step 16: Ways to Spell /k/ 85

Step 17: Long E Spelled EA 89

Step 18: Ways to Spell /ē/ 95

Step 19: Suffix ED 99

Step 20: The Drop the E Rule 105

Step 21: The /er/ of *First* 111

Step 22: Ways to Spell /er/ 115

Step 23: The Sound of /o͝o/ Spelled OO 119

Step 24: Three-Letter I 125

Step 25: Ways to Spell /ī/ 129

Step 26: The Change the Y to I Rule 133

Step 27: Contractions 139

Step 28: Homophones 145

3 Appendices

Appendix A: Phonograms Taught in Level Three 151

Appendix B: Scope and Sequence of Level Three 153

Appendix C: Words Taught in Level Three 155

1
Preparing for Level Three

Gather the Materials

Following is the list of materials you will need for teaching Level Three.

- ☐ Material Packet for Level Three
- ☐ Set of *All About Spelling* Letter Tiles
- ☐ Index card box
- ☐ Yellow colored pencil
- ☐ Lined notebook paper
- ☐ Rubber band (used in Step 27)

You will also need these items from your student's Level Two Spelling Review Box:

- ☐ Phonogram Cards 1-43
- ☐ Sound Cards 1-43
- ☐ Key Cards 1-9

These items are optional:

- ☐ Stickers or colored pencils for the Progress Chart
- ☐ Phonogram Audio CD-Rom (recommended)
- ☐ Letter tile magnets
- ☐ Magnet board

Set Up the Spelling Review Box

All About Spelling features continual, individualized review. This ensures that your students don't forget what you teach them and they get the practice they need in exactly the areas they need it. Flashcards help accomplish much of this review, and the Spelling Review Box keeps them all organized.

As in previous levels, four types of flashcards will be used:

 These yellow cards offer **visual and verbal review**: you hold up the card and your student says the sound(s) the phonogram makes. You have 43 Phonogram Cards from previous levels, and 10 new Phonogram Cards are included with Level Three.

 Each red flashcard offers **aural and tactile review**: you dictate the sound and your student listens and writes the letter(s) that make the sound. You have 43 Sound Cards from previous levels, and 16 new Sound Cards are included with Level Three.

 Each blue flashcard contains a rule or generalization about spelling. They are used during lessons to **reinforce new concepts**. You read and review these flashcards with your student. Your student's index card box should contain the Key Cards from previous levels plus the 10 new cards included with Level Three.

 Each green flashcard contains a word that students learn to spell in Level Three. These cards offer **aural, verbal, and tactile review**: you dictate the word and your student listens to, segments, and writes the word.

Here are the steps to set up the Spelling Review Box:

1. Locate the flashcard dividers in the Material Packet. Cut them apart and place them in the index card box in numerical order.

2. Cut apart the new Phonogram Cards, Sound Cards, Key Cards, and Word Cards. Put all flashcards behind the appropriate Future Lessons dividers.

3. Transfer all Phonogram Cards, Sound Cards, and Key Cards from Level Two into the Level Three index card box. Place them behind the appropriate Mastered dividers. These cards will continue to be reviewed to keep the concepts fresh in your student's mind.

Organize the Letter Tiles

We will continue to use the specially color-coded letter tiles to teach new spelling concepts.

Though many teachers set up the tiles on the table at the beginning of each lesson, others have opted to magnetize them and store them on a magnetic board. This is a great way to keep the tiles organized between lessons and to save time, too.

Here are tips for preparing and using magnetic tiles:

- If you purchased the precut magnetic strips from *All About Spelling*, simply peel off the paper backing and center the magnets on the back of each letter tile.

- Store the letter tiles on a magnet board. For recommendations on magnet boards, see www.all-about-spelling.com/letter-tile-magnets.html.

- You can work with the tiles right on the magnet board, or remove just the tiles you need for the lesson and arrange them on the table.

- Only letter tiles which have been introduced in the lessons should be stored on the board.

Here are the steps to organize the letter tiles in preparation for teaching Level Three:

1. If you magnetize the tiles: See the diagram in Step 1 for beginning tile set-up for Level Three, and arrange the tiles on the magnet board as shown. Tiles for later use should be stored as described below. Magnetize and add them to the board when indicated in the Steps.

2. If you do not magnetize the tiles: Label three Ziploc bags **Use Now**, **Use Later**, and **Save for Level Four**. Sort the letter tiles and labels into the appropriate bags, as shown below.

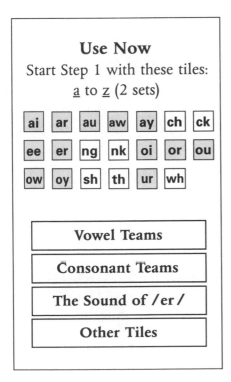

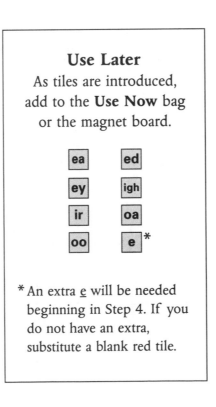

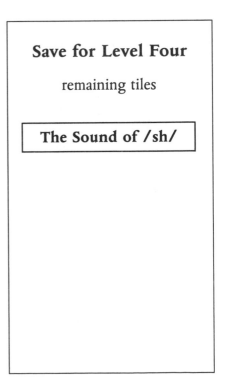

Take a Look at the Six Syllable Types

There are six different syllable types. So far, your student has learned how to spell words with the first five syllable types. Those will be reviewed, and then the sixth syllable type will be taught.

As a refresher, take a look at the syllable types:

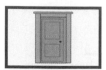 **Closed syllables** are represented by a closed door. In a closed syllable, the vowel is closed in by (that is, followed by) a consonant. In a closed syllable, the vowel is usually short. Examples of closed syllables include *bat, fish, and thim–*.

 **Open syllables** are represented by an open door. In an open syllable, the vowel is open; it is the last letter of the syllable and is usually long. Examples include *we, no, and ma–*.

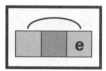 **Vowel-Consonant-E syllables** are represented by three letter tiles: a vowel, a consonant, and an e. The line from the e to the vowel signifies the silent e making the vowel before it long. Examples of this syllable type include *name, hope*, and *–ite*. In the lesson plans, Vowel-Consonant-E is often abbreviated as VCE.

 **Vowel Team syllables** are represented by a team of horses. Just as a team of horses works together, the two vowels in a Vowel Team syllable work together to make one sound. Examples of Vowel Team syllables include *toy, slow,* and *eat*.

 **R-controlled syllables** are represented by Cowboy R roping in the vowels. In this syllable type, the letter r controls the sound of the vowel before it, as in the phonograms or, ar, er, ur, ir, ear, and our. Examples of R-controlled syllables include *her, corn,* and *spar–*.

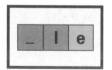 **C+le syllables** are represented by three letter tiles: a consonant, the letter l, and an e. Examples of C+le syllables include *–ble, –ple,* and *–tle*.

In Level Three, your student will learn how to add suffixes (such as *–ed, –ful, –ing, –ment*) and combine syllable types to create more multisyllable words. Without the knowledge gained through labeling syllable types, it can be confusing. Why do you double the p in *stepping* but not in *weeping*? Why do you need a double consonant in *little* but not in *maple*? When the student has a working knowledge of syllable types, the answers make perfect sense.

Cut apart the syllable tags. If you added magnets to the letter tiles, you will want to magnetize the syllable tags as well.

Review the Procedure for Spelling with Tiles

If you look ahead to the lesson plans, you will notice that the Spell with Tiles section is no longer included. Most students at this level can write the dictated words directly on paper. However, student ability varies widely, so you as the teacher are in the best position to decide whether your individual student would benefit from continuing to spell each new word with the letter tiles.

If you feel that your student still needs the hands-on work with letter tiles to establish good spelling habits and internalize the concepts taught in the lessons, review the illustrations below. The left column shows the procedure for spelling one-syllable words, which was taught in Level One. The right column shows the procedure for spelling multisyllable words. The two routines are slightly different, so coach your student through the proper method until it becomes habit for him.

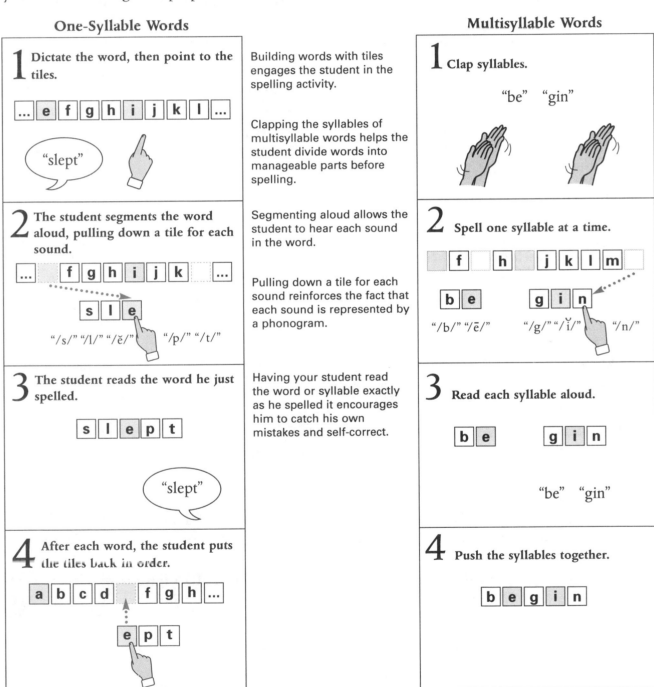

One-Syllable Words

1 Dictate the word, then point to the tiles.

… | e | f | g | h | i | j | k | l | …

"slept"

Building words with tiles engages the student in the spelling activity.

Clapping the syllables of multisyllable words helps the student divide words into manageable parts before spelling.

2 The student segments the word aloud, pulling down a tile for each sound.

… | f | g | h | i | j | k | …
s | l | e

"/s/" "/l/" "/ĕ/"   "/p/" "/t/"

Segmenting aloud allows the student to hear each sound in the word.

Pulling down a tile for each sound reinforces the fact that each sound is represented by a phonogram.

3 The student reads the word he just spelled.

s | l | e | p | t

"slept"

Having your student read the word or syllable exactly as he spelled it encourages him to catch his own mistakes and self-correct.

4 After each word, the student puts the tiles back in order.

a | b | c | d | f | g | h | …
e | p | t

Multisyllable Words

1 Clap syllables.

"be" "gin"

2 Spell one syllable at a time.

f | h | j | k | l | m
b | e   g | i | n

"/b/" "/ē/"   "/g/" "/ĭ/" "/n/"

3 Read each syllable aloud.

b | e   g | i | n

"be" "gin"

4 Push the syllables together.

b | e | g | i | n

Learn How to Handle Troublemakers

Troublemakers are words that, for one reason or another, are challenging to spell. They tend to fall into one of these categories: words with careless mistakes, mispronounced words, and words that don't follow the spelling rules.

To tame these troublemakers, you need to match the problem with the correct remedy. Figure out why the student is misspelling the word, and then correct the problem by using one or more of the following strategies:

1. **The student misspells a word you think he should be able to spell.** For example, your student writes down the word *form* instead of *from*, and you know that he has spelled this word correctly on other occasions. Ask him to slowly read exactly what he wrote down. Make sure that he reads each phonogram. Many times, the student will catch and correct his own mistake. If he doesn't see his mistake, tell him, "You wrote *form*, but we want the word *from*. What do you need to change?"

2. **The student's pronunciation of a word makes it difficult to spell.** If a student learns to pronounce a word clearly, he will usually be able to spell it correctly. Some words that are commonly mispronounced and misspelled are *probably* (*probly*), *secretary* (*secertary*), *because* (*becuz*), and *library* (*libary*). Model the correct pronunciation of the word, and have your student segment the word syllable by syllable.

   Some words are not pronounced clearly in everyday speech. For example, most Americans pronounce the word *button* as *butn* and *little* as *liddle*. The vowel sound in the unaccented syllable gets lost in the normal rhythm of speech. In these cases, it is helpful to "pronounce for spelling" and enunciate each syllable clearly and as it is written. Regional accents can also make certain words more challenging. If your student pronounces *forget* as *ferget*, remind him to "pronounce for spelling." This technique was taught in *All About Spelling Level One* and will be used throughout the series.

3. **The student forgot a rule or generalization.** If this is the case, pull out the related Key Card and review the concept. Demonstrate the rule by using the letter tiles to spell the troublesome word. Keep the Key Card behind the Review divider for daily practice until your student demonstrates mastery of that concept.

4. **The misspelled word is a Rule Breaker.** A Rule Breaker is a word that does not follow the rules of spelling. For example, in the word *said*, we expect the <u>ai</u> to say /ā/, not /ĕ/. Each time the student encounters a Rule Breaker, the lesson plans direct him to circle the letters that don't follow the rules and throw the Word Card into jail.

   If your student misspells the Rule Breaker at a later date, have him follow these steps:
   - Look at the Word Card, and then look at an empty spot on the table.
   - Picture the word on the table, and spell the word aloud three times.
   - With his finger, write the word on the table in VERY BIG LETTERS three times.
   - Spell the word on paper three times.
   - Then throw the Rule Breaker back in jail.

   To prepare for the lessons, find the jail in the Material Packet. Cut out the spaces between the jail bars so that the Rule Breaker can peek through.

Meet the New Teaching Tools

Now it's time to take a look at the other materials that are included in the Material Packet. Some will look familiar, like the Word Banks, Syllable Tags, Syllable Division Rules Chart, and the Jail. Level Three also includes some new tools to help you present the lessons clearly and to help your student learn through verbal, visual, and tactile means.

For now, you may wish to store the remaining items in a large manila envelope. This way, when they are called for in the "You will need" section of a Step, you will know right where to find them. Complete instructions for their use will be provided in the lesson plans.

If you are curious about the new materials, here is a sneak peak:

 **New for Level Three**

In Level Three you will find several new activities and tools that will help your student internalize new concepts. Look for the **New!** flag for tips on how to use the materials and for additional information on activities.

Silent E Book	Previous levels introduced some of the jobs of silent e. In Level Three, your student will learn the final jobs of silent e and use his detective skills to **identify and categorize** them in the Silent E Book.
Homophones List	The Homophones List is an ongoing activity that will introduce the student to homophone pairs. Whenever a new pair is taught, the student will enter the words on the list. This activity ensures that your student will be able to **identify and use the correct word** in his writing.
Suffix Tiles	In addition to the letter tiles, your student will be using suffix tiles to build words. The suffixes offer **visual and tactile** practice for the student to help him recognize and correctly use suffixes.
1-1-1 Rule Card	The 1-1-1 Rule Card helps your student decide when to double the consonant when adding vowel suffixes. Using the card to build words gives the student **visual reinforcement** of the rule.
ED Word Sheet	Your student will be working extensively with suffixes. The ED Word Sheet will help him **identify** past tense words and the three sounds of ed, then **sort and categorize** words under the correct sound.

2

Complete Step-by-Step
Lesson Plans

Step 1 - Warming Up

This is a fast-paced review of concepts taught in previous levels. Your student will also learn the ai, ay, and ur phonograms.

You will need: Phonogram Cards 1-46, Sound Cards 1-46, syllable tags, Syllable Division Rules Chart, letter tiles ai, ay, and ur, stickers or colored pencils, progress chart

For each lesson, arrange the letter tiles as shown below, adding new tiles when indicated.

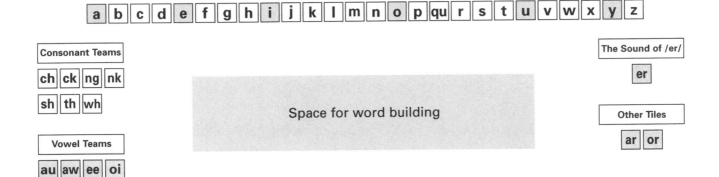

Consonant Teams				The Sound of /er/
ch	ck	ng	nk	er
sh	th	wh		

Space for word building

Vowel Teams				Other Tiles
au	aw	ee	oi	ar	or
ou	ow	oy		

Review

Review Phonogram Cards 1-43

Do a brisk review of Phonogram Cards 1-43 from the previous levels. Hold up each card and have your student say the sound(s) of the phonogram. Place the cards that your student has mastered behind the Mastered divider. Cards that your student should review again go behind the Review divider.

Review Sound Cards 1-43

Review Sound Cards 1-43 from the previous levels. Dictate the sound(s) and have your student write the letter or letter combination that makes the sound(s). He should say the sound as he writes the phonogram. Sort behind the Mastered and Review dividers.

Analyze Words

Take out the syllable tags. Set the **C+le** tag aside for a future lesson.

Build the words shown below and ask the accompanying questions.

| c | o | d | e |

"Read this word." *Code.*

"What is the first sound in the word *code*?" */k/.*

"Why do we spell the /k/ sound with a c̲, and not a k̲?" *We always try a c̲ first.*

"Is the o̲ long or short?" *Long.*

"What makes it long?" *Silent e̲.*

"Label the syllable." *Student uses the **VCE** tag.*

| k | ee | p |

"What is the first sound in the word *keep*?" */k/.*

"Why do we spell it with a k̲, and not a c̲?" *Because a c̲ would be soft here. (A c̲ would say /s/ because of the e̲.)*

"How many sounds are in the word *keep*?" *Three.*

"But I see four letters. How can that be?" *Two letters make one sound.*

"Label the syllable." *Student uses the **Vowel Team** tag.*

| c | e | n | t |

"What sound does c̲ have in this word?" */s/.*

"Why is the c̲ soft?" *Because of the e̲.*

"C̲ says /s/ before what three letters?" *E̲, i̲, and y̲.*

"Is the e̲ long or short?" *Short.*

"Label the syllable." *Student uses the **Closed** syllable tag.*

| l | ar | g | e |

"Read this word." *Large.*

"What is the last sound in the word *large*?" */j/.*

"Why don't we spell the /j/ sound with a j̲?" *English words don't end in j̲.*

"Why does the g say /j/?" *Because of the e̲.*

"What three letters can make g soft?" *E̲, i̲, or y̲.*

"Label the syllable." *Student uses the **R-controlled** tag.*

| t | ar | g | e | t |

"Does g always say /j/ before e̲, i̲, or y̲?" *No, not always.*

"Read this word." *Target.*

"Is the e̲ long or short in this word?" *Short.*

Review
(continued)

d e s k "Read this word." *Desk.*

"Segment this word." */d/–/ĕ/–/s/–/k/.*

"What is the last sound in this word?" */k/.*

"Why can't we spell the /k/ sound with a <u>ck</u>?" *We only use <u>ck</u> after a short vowel.*

"Make this word plural." *Student adds an <u>s</u>.*

g l a s s "Read this word." *Glass.*

"How many syllables are in the word *glass?*" *One.*

"Does this word have a single vowel?" *Yes.*

"What three letters are often doubled after a single vowel?" *<u>F</u>, <u>l</u>, and <u>s</u>.*

"Make this word plural." *Student adds <u>e</u>-<u>s</u>.*

m i n d "Read this word." *Mind.*

"Is the <u>i</u> long or short?" *Long.*

"Why?" *An <u>i</u> can be long when it comes before two consonants.*

f l y "Read this word." *Fly.*

"What is the last sound?" */ī/.*

"In this word, why don't we spell the sound of /ī/ with the letter <u>i</u>?" *English words don't end in <u>i</u>.*

"Is the <u>y</u> a vowel or consonant here?" *Vowel.*

Review Syllable Division Rules

Take out the Syllable Division Rules Chart. Cover Rule #4 because that has not yet been taught. Read through Rules #1, 2, and 3 with your student.

Build the following words and have your student divide them into syllables.

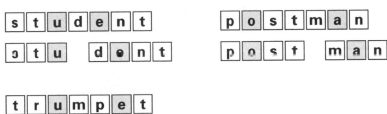

New Teaching

Teach New Phonograms AY, AI, and UR

"We have three new tiles today."

Point to the a̲y̲ tile. ay

"This tile says /ā/, two-letter /ā/ that we **may** use at the end of **English words**. Repeat after me: /ā/, two-letter /ā/ that we may use at the end of English words." *Student repeats.*

Point to the a̲i̲ tile. ai

"This tile says /ā/, two-letter /ā/ that we **may not** use at the end of **English words**. Repeat after me: /ā/, two-letter /ā/ that we may not use at the end of English words." *Student repeats.*

"Why can't we use this tile at the end of English words?" *Because English words don't end in i̲.*

Point to the u̲r̲ tile. ur

"This tile says /er/ as in *nurse*. Repeat after me: /er/ as in *nurse*." *Student repeats.*

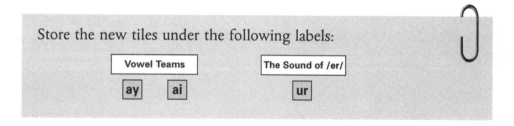

Store the new tiles under the following labels:

Vowel Teams — ay ai

The Sound of /er/ — ur

Take out Phonogram Cards 44-46 and practice them with your student.

Practice Sound Cards 44-46 with your student. Dictate the sound and have your student write the phonogram.

File the cards behind the appropriate Review divider in your index card box.

Reinforcement

Dictate Sentences

Dictate several sentences each day. The sentences for this review lesson contain words that were taught in Levels 1 and 2.

The lake is frozen in winter.

Dan made the bed.

Zip up your backpack.

We sang camp songs at dark.

The old bikes must be broken.

Jim saw the dentist.

Our garden is huge.

My glasses got broken.

Aunt Beth found her cute brown dog.

The path was dark.

She felt a cobweb on her face.

Do you see the green frog?

Ron wishes he had a small tiger.

The soil in my garden is black.

Have a thick slice of ham.

She hid behind the tree.

Give the cake to Jim.

Her sister is tall.

Why did Tom quit the game?

Do not fly kites in a storm!

Say the sentence only once! Your student should repeat the sentence before he begins writing. By saying the words out loud, he will remember them much more easily and will be able to write them down accurately.

Mark the Progress Chart

After each lesson has been mastered, have your student color in or place a sticker over that Step number on the chart.

Step 2 – Vowel Teams AI and AY

This lesson will teach words containing the sound of /ā/ spelled ai and ay.

You will need: Word Bank for AI/AY, Word Cards 1-10

Review

Phonogram Cards   Sound Cards   Key Cards

Word Analysis

 "Read this word." *Enjoy.*

New! A new feature in Level Three is Word Analysis, which you'll find at the beginning of every lesson.

This section reviews previously learned concepts to help keep them fresh in your student's mind.

"What is the first sound in this word?" */ĕ/.*

"Is that the short sound of e or the long sound of e?" *Short.*

"Divide this word into syllables." *Student divides between the two consonants.*

"Why can't I spell this first syllable with just an n?" *That would say /n/, not /ĕn/. Every syllable must have a vowel.*

"What is the last sound in this word?" */oy/.*

"Why can't I use oi for the sound of oy?" *English words don't end in i.*

"Label the syllables." *Student uses the **Closed** and **Vowel Team** tags.*

New Teaching

Teach Two More Ways to Spell /ā/

Build the words *apron* and *same*. a p r o n   s a m e

"You have learned several ways to spell the sound of /ā/. Let's look at two of the ways."

New Teaching
(continued)

Divide the word *apron* into syllables. **a**   **p** **r** **o** **n**

"Why is the a̲ long in the word *apron*?" *Because it is at the end of a syllable.*

"Good. The first way to spell the sound of /ā/ is to put it in an open syllable."

Point to the word *same*. "Why is the a̲ long in the word *same*?" *Because of the silent e̲.*

"Right. The second way to spell the sound of /ā/ is to add a silent e̲."

"You have also learned two other phonograms that make the sound of /ā/. Pull down those tiles." *Student pulls down the a̲i̲ and a̲y̲ tiles.*

ai   **ay**

"Today we will work on spelling words with the sound of /ā/ spelled a̲i̲ and a̲y̲."

"Which of these tiles can be used at the end of a word?" *A̲y.*

"Good. When you hear the sound of /ā/ at the **end** of a word, it is usually spelled a̲y̲, as in the word *day*."

d **ay**

"Change *day* to *pay*." *Student exchanges the d̲ for a p̲.*

Have your student spell these words with tiles:

play   **clay**   **say**   **stay**   **spray**

Build the word *today* with tiles. **t** **o** **d** **ay**

"What does this word say?" *Today.*

"Good. When you spell this word, 'pronounce it for spelling.' Pronounce it clearly: *tōō-day*."

Point to the a̲i̲ tile. "This tile is used to spell the sound of /ā/ in the **middle** of a word."

"Why would this tile **not** be used at the end of a word?" *Because English words don't end in i̲.*

Build the word *rain*. **r** **ai** **n**

Step 2: Vowel Teams AI and AY

New Teaching
(continued)

Point to the <u>ai</u> tile. "<u>Ai</u> is used to spell the /ā/ sound in the word *rain*. It is also used to spell the sound of /ā/ in these next words."

Have your student spell these words with tiles:

jail   **wait**   **fail**   **trail**

Introduce the Word Bank for AI/AY

Have your student read through the **Word Bank for AI/AY** to improve visual memory. There are several ways to spell the sound of /ā/, and we want students to become very familiar with the words in this Word Bank. This will enable the student to recognize the correct spelling of long <u>a</u> when he needs to spell one of these words.

Word Cards 1-10: Spell on Paper

Dictate the words and have your student spell them on paper. The student should write one word per line.

If a spelling **Tip!** word has a homophone—another word that sounds alike but is spelled differently—dictate the word in a sentence. The student does not write the sentence.

1. play

2. paint

3. way   Come this way.

4. fair   The game wasn't fair!

5. stay

6. say

7. rain   Do you like the rain?

8. train

9. mail   Did you get the mail?

10. today

Place Word Cards 1-10 behind the Review divider.

Reinforcement

More Words

clay	**day**	**fail**	**jail**
mailbox	**May**	**pay**	**pray**
ray	**sail**	**snail**	**spray**
tail (animal tail)	**trail**	**tray**	**wait**

Reinforcement
(continued)

Dictate Sentences
Dictate several sentences each day.

Did your sister say she will go?

Stay here until the rain stops.

We will take the train.

A tree fell across the trail.

Did you get the mail today?

It was a long way home.

Jill has a part in the play.

Will you play with me?

The cat has a short tail.

Wet paint is on the wall.

Was that a fair game?

Mike will pay the bill.

Step 2: Vowel Teams AI and AY

Step 3 – Ways to Spell /ā/

In this lesson, your student will analyze four ways to spell the sound of /ā/.

You will need: Sound Card 47

Review

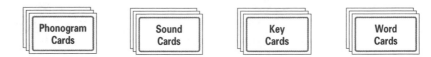

Have your student read through **Word Bank for AI/AY.**

Word Analysis

| b | r | a | k | e | s |

"How many sounds are in the word *brakes*?" *Five.*

"What is the job of the silent *e*?" *To make the a long.*

"What would this word say if I left out the *e*?" */brăks/.*

"Why can't I use a *ck* for the /k/ sound?" *Ck is used only after a short vowel sound.*

"How many syllables?" *One.*

"Label the syllable." *Student uses the VCE tag.*

New Teaching

Introduce the Word Sort for /ā/ Chart

Write these four headings across the top of lined paper. Draw vertical lines to form four columns:

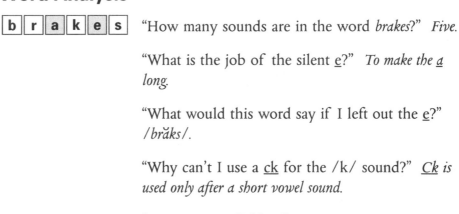

a	a–e	ai	ay

Point to the column headings. "Here are four ways to spell the sound of /ā/."

New Teaching
(continued)

Give your student a new sheet of lined paper. "I will dictate a word, and you will write it down on your paper. When you are satisfied that you have spelled the word correctly, copy the word to the correct column on this chart."

Dictate these words:

April	**same**	**say**	**paper**	**rain**
play	**late**	**grape**	**wait**	**made**

"How did you spell the sound of /ā/ at the end of a word?" _Ay_.

> **New!** The Word Sort activity is preparation for learning more difficult words in higher levels. It will give your student another strategy for spelling words. If he can't recall the spelling of a word, he should test out various ways of spelling the sound and choose which one looks right. This is one more skill that will enable him to become a strong independent speller.

Teach Sound Card 47

"Today we have a new Sound Card."

Read Sound Card 47:

New! This is the first of the six new "summary" Sound Cards introduced in Level Three.

When you review this new type of card, you will ask your student how to spell a sound, and he will write down all the ways he has learned to spell that sound.

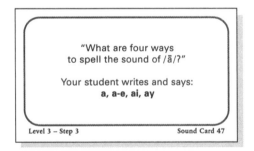

"What are four ways
to spell the sound of /ā/?"

Your student writes and says:
a, a-e, ai, ay

Level 3 – Step 3   Sound Card 47

Since this is a new type of Sound Card, demonstrate for your student how he should respond to the question: "Write and say the four ways like this."

Say the name of the letters as you write them down: "a, a-consonant-e, ai, ay." Explain that we write a _dash_ for the word _consonant_.

Practice this Sound Card with your student, and then store it behind the Review divider.

New Teaching
(continued)

More spellings of long <u>a</u> include:
- <u>ea</u> as in *steak*
- <u>ei</u> as in *their*
- <u>eigh</u> as in *weigh*
- <u>ey</u> as in *they*

These spellings aren't used in nearly as many words as the four we studied today and will be covered at a later time.

Reinforcement

Dictate Sentences

Dictate several sentences each day.

We will play a game in the rain.

The snail left a wet trail.

The flame is like a ray of sun.

Do you want to trade?

I made a face at Sam!

It is late in the day.

Ed ate all the cake!

My mailbox is by the gate.

She is safe on home base!

Did you spray the clay with water?

I like to sail in May.

My cat can wave her tail so fast!

Step 4 – Silent E Book

In this lesson, your student will begin the Silent E Book and learn to identify the jobs of silent e.

You will need: Silent E Book, third e letter tile (or substitute a blank red tile)

Review

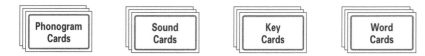

Word Bank for AI/AY

Word Analysis

quite

"How do we spell the sound of /kw/ at the beginning of a word?" *Qu.*

"Is the i long or short?" *Long.*

"Why is it long?" *Because of the silent e.*

"Read this word." *Quite.*

"How many vowel sounds do you hear?" *One.*

"Does the u act like a vowel here?" *No.*

"What would it say if we removed the silent e?" *Quit.*

"Label the syllable." *Student uses the VCE tag.*

New Teaching

New! The Silent E Book will help your student recognize, categorize, and internalize the jobs of silent e.

Introduce Silent E Book

Give your student the Silent E Book. "You have learned that silent e has several different jobs. You will keep track of these jobs in this book."

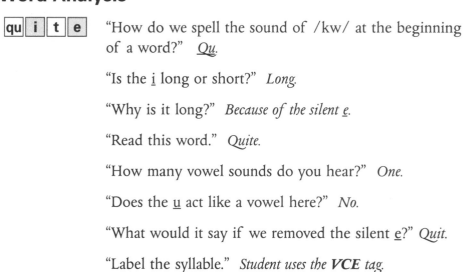

New Teaching
(continued)

Have your student write his name on the cover.

Read the headings on pages 1-3 with your student.

"When you learn a word that has a silent e, you will add it to this book. Keep your eyes open for silent e words."

Build the word *plate*.   p l a t e

"What is this word?" *Plate.*

"What is the job of silent e?" *It makes the a long* (or, *it makes the vowel say its name*).

Turn to page 1 in the Silent E Book. Have your student write in the word *plate* on line 2.

Build the words *fence* and *large*.   f e n c e   l ar g e

Point to the word *fence*. "What does this word say?" *Fence.*

"What is the job of silent e in this word?" *It makes the c soft.*

Point to the word *large*. "What does this word say?" *Large.*
"What is the job of silent e in this word?" *It makes the g soft.*

Turn to page 2 in the Silent E Book. Have your student write in the words *fence* and *large* on lines 3 and 4.

Build the words *clue* and *give*.   c l u e   g i v e

Point to the word *clue*. "What is this word?" *Clue.*

"What is the job of silent e in this word?" *It keeps u from being the last letter in a word.*

Point to the word *give*. "What is this word?" *Give.*

"What is the job of silent e in this word?" *It keeps v from being the last letter in a word.*

Turn to page 3 and have your student write in the words *clue* and *give*.

Build the word *ice*.   i c e

"Sometimes silent e has two jobs. See if you can find them in this word." *E makes i long and makes c soft.*

Have your student write the word *ice* on pages 1 and 2.

New Teaching
(continued)

Answer Key

twelve: pg. 3

smile: pg. 1

since: pg. 2

glue: pg. 3

hinge: pg. 2

hide: pg. 1

size: pg. 1

"When you spell a word with silent e, I want you to be a detective and figure out which job the silent e is doing."

Have the student place the following words in the correct section of the Silent E Book:

twelve	**smile**	**since**	**glue**	**hinge**
hide	**size**			

Some students add silent e to words that do not need it! This step of identifying the job of silent e will prevent the indiscriminate use of silent e. Allow your student to refer to the Silent E Book, if necessary, to remind himself of the jobs of silent e.

"Today we covered the first three jobs of silent e. We'll cover another job in the next lesson."

Reinforcement

Dictate Sentences

Dictate several sentences each day.

> **Did you glue those five plates?**
> **I made a hole in the ice.**
> **The queen bee is safe in her hive.**
> **I have quite a large face!**
> **Bob gave me a ride.**
> **Here is the blue fence.**
> **The dog cannot hide in his wire cage.**
> **I hope we can live in space one day!**
> **That huge place is on fire.**
> **Can you race for nine miles?**
> **The pile of rope is on the stage.**
> **I will carve my name in the tree.**

Step 5 – C+le Syllable Type, Part 1

Your student will learn the sixth syllable type and how to spell words containing C+le syllables. Your student will also learn the fourth job of silent e.

You will need: C+le syllable tag, Syllable Division Rules Chart, yellow pencil, jail, Word Cards 11-20

Review

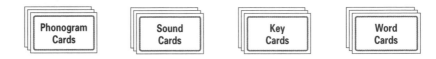

Word Analysis

| b | e | c | a | m | e |

"Divide the word *became* into syllables." *Student divides before the c.*

"What is the sound of the first letter?"   */b/.*

"What is the sound of the first e?"   */ē/.*

"Why is it long?"   *The e is at the end of a syllable.*

"What is the sound of the second e?"   *It is silent.*

"What is the job of the silent e?"   *To make the a long.*

"What letter says /k/ in this word?"   *C.*

"Why didn't I use a k there?"   *Use a c whenever you can. You only use a k if you can't use a c.*

"Label the syllable types."   *Student uses the **Open** and **VCE** tags.*

New Teaching

Teach the C+le Syllable Type

Take out the syllable tags.

Build the word *table*. | t | a | b | l | e |

"This word says *table*."

New Teaching
(continued)

Divide the word into two syllables: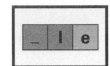

"Is the first syllable open or closed?" *Open, because nothing comes after the a.*

"Good. Place the correct syllable tag over the first syllable." *Student uses the **Open** syllable tag.*

Point to the second syllable. "This is a new syllable type."

"There is a consonant…" (point to the b) "…followed by l-e" (point to the l-e). "The e is silent."

"We call this a **consonant l-e syllable**."

Take out the C+le syllable tag.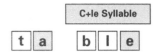

"We use the **consonant l-e syllable** tag to label this new type of syllable. The blue tile represents a consonant, and the letter tiles for l and e follow." Place the C+le syllable tag over the second syllable.

"This syllable type is used in many words. Listen for the /l/ sound at the end of these words: *single, uncle, sample, tickle.*"

Silent E Book: Teach the Fourth Job of Silent E

"I want to spell the word *maple*. First I pull down the tiles for the first syllable: /mā/."

m a

"Then I spell the second syllable: /pl/."

m a   p l e

"The e is silent in a **consonant l-e syllable**. Remember that every syllable must have a vowel. The e is there so that this syllable has a vowel." Push the two syllables together.

"This is the fourth job of silent e." Turn to page 4 in the Silent E Book and have your student write in the word *maple* on line 2.

Step 5: C+le Syllable Type, Part 1

New Teaching
(continued)

Teach Syllable Division Rule #4

"When a word ends in **consonant l-e**, we can divide it into syllables by **counting back three tiles**."

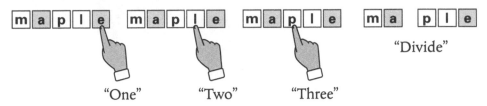

"One"   "Two"   "Three"   "Divide"

Take out the Syllable Division Rules Chart. "This is the fourth syllable division rule." Read Rule #4 with your student.

Build the word *handle*. | h | a | n | d | l | e |

"Count back three tiles to divide this word." *Student divides the word.*

"Label the syllables." *Student labels the syllables.*

| Closed Syllable | | C+le Syllable |

| h | a | n | | d | l | e |

"What does this word say?" *Handle.*

Teach a Rule Breaker

Build the word *said*. | s | ai | d |

"This word is *said*. What letters don't say the sound we expect them to say?" *The ai.*

Show Word Card 20 to your student.

said

Level 3 – Step 5   Word Card 20

"Circle the ai in this word, because it doesn't make the sound we expect it to make." Have your student fill in the circle with yellow pencil.

"The word *said* is a Rule Breaker. We throw Rule Breakers in jail!" *Student puts the card behind the jail bars.*

"Spell the word *said*." *Student spells the word.*

Word Cards 11-20: Spell on Paper

Dictate the words and have your student spell them on paper.

11. table
12. candle
13. title
14. maple
15. able
16. uncle
17. staple
18. gentle
19. handle
20. said

Place Word Cards 11-20 behind the Review divider.

Reinforcement

Dictate Sentences

Dictate several sentences each day.

Why is a pig at the table?

The candle left wax on my desk.

I like the title of that song.

That maple tree is tall.

She is able to play the trumpet.

My uncle Ted has three ducks.

I put a staple at the top of the page.

Be gentle with the glass doll!

I broke the handle on the cup.

Beth said that you are a sweet boy!

The wild owl made me smile.

Do you need a red pencil?

Step 6 – C+le Syllable Type, Part 2

This lesson will teach one new phonogram and when to double the consonant before the C+le syllable, and will introduce the concept of homophones.

You will need: letter tile *oa*, Phonogram Card 47, Sound Card 48, Key Card 10, Homophones List, Word Cards 21-30

Review

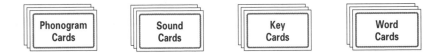

Word Analysis

| l | aw | "How many sounds do you hear in the word *law*?" *Two.*

"What are the two sounds?" */l/–/aw/.*

"What is another way to spell the sound of /aw/?" *Au.*

"*Au* is another way to spell the sound of /aw/. Why can't I use that spelling here?" *Because English words don't end in u.*

"Label this syllable." *Student uses the **Vowel Team** tag.*

New Teaching

Teach New Phonogram OA

"We have a new tile today." **oa**

"This tile says **/ō/, two-letter /ō/ that we may not use at the end of English words.** Repeat after me: /ō/, two-letter /ō/ that we <u>may not</u> use at the end of English words." *Student repeats.*

Store the new tile under the following label:

Vowel Teams

oa

New Teaching
(continued)

Take out Phonogram Card 47 and practice it with your student.

Practice Sound Card 48 with your student. Dictate the sound and have your student write the phonogram.

File the cards behind the appropriate Review dividers in the index card box.

Introduce the Concept of Doubling the Consonant

Build the word *little* with letter tiles.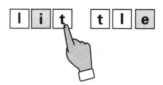

"Here is a word that uses the **consonant l-e** syllable type. Divide this word into syllables." *Student counts back three letters and divides.*

"When we say this word, *little*, it sounds like the first syllable is /lĭ/. We don't hear this t." Point to the t.

"We use this t to close the syllable, even though we don't hear it."

Take away the first t.   l i   t l e

"If we don't have two t's, what would this word say?" /lī/-/tl/. *The i would be long because it would be in an open syllable.*

"Right. When you hear a short vowel, it is **usually** in a closed syllable."

> This generalization works **most** of the time. There are words where this doesn't work, such as *city*.   **Tip!**

"Spell this word with tiles, using a consonant l-e syllable: *apple*." *Student spells with letter tiles.*

a p p l e

If student doesn't double the p, lead him to see that the word would say /ā/–/pl/: Tip!

1. Have him divide the word into syllables (count back three, then divide).

    | a | | p | l | e |

2. Ask him to read the resulting word. The first syllable is open, and would say /ā/ instead of /ă/.

3. Explain that he needs to close the first syllable so the a can say /ă/.

Practice this concept with the following words:

middle   **giggle**   **puddle**   **puzzle**

Label Syllable Types

Build the following words with letter tiles. Have your student divide the words into syllables and label with the proper syllable tag:

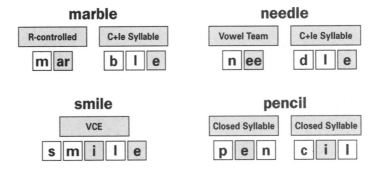

marble

| R-controlled | | C+le Syllable |
| m | ar | b | l | e |

needle

| Vowel Team | | C+le Syllable |
| n | ee | d | l | e |

smile

| VCE |
| s | m | i | l | e |

pencil

| Closed Syllable | Closed Syllable |
| p | e | n | c | i | l |

Silent E Book: Identify the Job of Silent E

Have your student enter these words on the correct page of his Silent E Book:

apple (pg. 4)   **trade** (pg. 1)   **have** (pg. 3)

Introduce the Homophones *Four* and *For*

Build the word *four*.   f | ou | r

"This is the word *four*, like the number *four*. Which letters are working together to make the /ō/ sound?" *Ou*.

Have your student write the word *four* on his paper, followed by the numeral 4.

"You already know another word that sounds the same but is spelled differently."

Build the word *for*.   f | or

"*For*, as in, *this present is for you*."

Teach Key Card 10: Homophones

"Two words that sound alike but are spelled differently are called **homophones**. Repeat this word: **homophones**." *Student repeats the word*.

Read Key Card 10 with your student and file behind the Review divider.

Start the Homophones List

Take out the Homophones List. "When you learn a new pair of homophones, write it on this Homophones List. Today you will write in the words *for* and *four*." *Student writes* for *and* four *on the first line of the Homophones List*.

Step 6: C+le Syllable Type, Part 2

New Teaching
(continued)

"Now I'll say a sentence, and you point to the correct spelling of *four/for* on your Homophones List."

Read the following sentences and make sure your student points to the correct word on the Homophones List:

My little brother is <u>four</u> years old.
This phone call is <u>for</u> you.
Use baking soda <u>for</u> your experiment.
<u>Four</u> turtles were sunning themselves on a log.

Word Cards 21-30: Spell on Paper

Dictate the words and have your student spell them on paper.

21. little
22. middle
23. apple
24. bubble
25. giggle
26. needle
27. puzzle
28. puddle
29. marble
30. four   I have four marbles.

Place Word Cards 21-30 behind the Review divider.

> Are any words giving your student trouble? If so, review the article "Learn How to Handle Troublemakers" on page 8.
>
> **Tip!**
>
> After a word has been misspelled and subsequently corrected, dictate the word later in the spelling lesson. Come back to it several times that day, and write a note to yourself to review that word again the next day.
>
> Customizing your student's instruction in this way will help his spelling ability grow more quickly.

Reinforcement

Dictate Sentences

Dictate several sentences each day.

Ben kept the little frog in his bathtub.

I swim in the middle of the lake.

I love green apples!

The water is full of bubbles.

Your jokes make me giggle.

The shark has a nose like a needle.

Can you do this puzzle?

Sue sat in the mud puddle.

Will you trade that marble with me?

That bug has four wings.

The path was dark.

I wish that windmill was mine.

Step 6: C+le Syllable Type, Part 2

Step 7 – The /er/ of *Nurse*

This lesson will teach words with the second most common spelling of the sound of /er/: ur. It will also teach the fifth job of silent e.

You will need: Word Bank for UR, Word Cards 31-40

Review

Word Bank for AI/AY

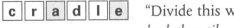

Are you remembering to shuffle the Word Cards before dictating them? Dictate review words with a variety of patterns.

Word Analysis

"Divide this word into syllables." *Student counts back three tiles and divides.*

"Is the a long or short?" *Long.*

"Why is it long?" *It is at the end of a syllable. It is open.*

"What does the first syllable say?" */crā/.*

"What does the second syllable say?" */dl/.*

"What is the job of the silent e?" *To add a vowel to the syllable.*

"Label the syllables." *Student uses **Open** and **C+le** tags.*

Teach Another Way to Spell /er/

Build the word *hunger*.

"You have learned the most common way to spell the sound of /er/. Point to the letter tile that spells the sound of /er/ in this word." *Student points to the er tile.*

"Good. You have also learned another phonogram that makes the sound of /er/. Pull down that tile." *Student pulls down the ur tile.*

"Today we will work on spelling words with the sound of /er/ spelled ur."

Build the word *burn*.

"What does this word say?" *Burn.*

"Good. I will dictate some words. The /er/ sound in these words is also spelled with the ur tile."

Dictate the following words:

| fur | turn | hurt | return |

Introduce the Word Bank for UR

> There are six basic phonograms that have the sound of /er/. They are each used in this sentence:
> H<u>er</u> n<u>ur</u>se f<u>ir</u>st w<u>or</u>ks <u>ear</u>ly (on the) j<u>our</u>ney.
> <u>Ur</u> is the second most common spelling of /er/.
>
> Since there are multiple ways to spell the sound of /er/, we will continue introducing just one of the spellings at a time. We will also give your student exercises to build up his visual memory of these words.

Have your student read through the **Word Bank for UR** to improve visual memory. We want students to become very familiar with the words in this Word Bank before the next spelling for /er/ is introduced.

Label Syllable Types

Build the following words with letter tiles. Have your student divide the words into syllables and label with the proper syllable tag:

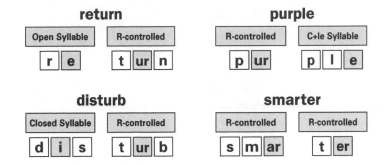

return

Open Syllable	R-controlled
r e	t ur n

purple

R-controlled	C+le Syllable
p ur	p l e

disturb

Closed Syllable	R-controlled
d i s	t ur b

smarter

R-controlled	R-controlled
s m ar	t er

Silent E Book: Teach the Fifth Job of Silent E

Build the word *are* with tiles.

ar e

Point to the <u>ar</u> tile. "What does this tile say?" /ar/.

"Good. This word says *are*. The <u>e</u> is silent."

Take out the Silent E Book. "Let's see if we can figure out which page the word *are* goes on." Help your student realize that the job of the silent <u>e</u> doesn't fall under any of the first four categories.

"If the job of silent <u>e</u> doesn't fit into any of the first four categories, we call it a **Handyman E,** because it helps out when the other silent <u>e</u>'s can't."

Have your student add these words to the Silent E Book:

are (pg. 5)   **curve** (pg. 3)   **middle** (pg. 4)   **these** (pg. 1)

New Teaching
(continued)

Word Cards 31-40: Spell on Paper

Dictate the words and have your student spell them on paper.

31. **turn**
32. **burn**
33. **curve**
34. **hurt**
35. **curl**
36. **return**
37. **church**
38. **fur**   The rabbit has soft fur.
39. **disturb**
40. **are**

Place Word Cards 31-40 behind the Review divider.

Reinforcement

More Words

purple

Dictate Sentences

Dictate several sentences each day.

It is your turn to play the game.
Do not burn the rice!
Run to the curve in the path.
I hurt my left leg.
Curl up on the carpet.
Return the sheep to the barn.
Pam went to church.
The pup has soft fur with spots.
Did I disturb your sleep?
Are you stuck in quicksand?
The farm is on the hill.
That purple pen is mine.

Step 7: The /er/ of *Nurse*

Step 8 – Y Can Say /ē/

In this lesson, your student will learn the most common spelling for /ē/ at the end of a word.

You will need: Key Card 11, Word Cards 41-50

Review

Phonogram Cards   Sound Cards   Key Cards   Word Cards

Word Bank for UR

Word Analysis

p l ow   "Read this word." *Plow.*

"What is the last sound in *plow.*" */ow/.*

"What is another way to spell the sound of /ow/?" *Ou.*

"How do I know that I can't use <u>ou</u> in this word?" *English words don't end in <u>u</u>.*

"Label the syllable." *Student uses the **Vowel Team** tag.*

New Teaching

Teach Another Way to Spell /ē/

Build the words *sheet, we,* and *eve.*

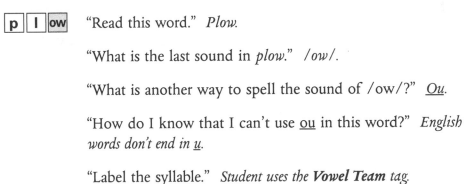

sh ee t   w e   e v e

"You have learned several ways to spell the sound of /ē/."

"Look at these three words. Point to the vowel team that spells the sound of /ē/." *Student points to the vowel team <u>ee</u> tile in the word* sheet.

Point to the word *we.* "Why is the <u>e</u> long in the word *we?*" *Because it is in an open syllable.*

New Teaching
(continued)

Point to the word *eve*. "Why is the e long in the word *eve*?" *Because of the silent e.*

"Good. You have also learned another phonogram that makes the sound of /ē/. Pull down that tile." *Student pulls down the y tile.*

"Today we will work on spelling words with the sound of /ē/ spelled y."

"What is the last sound you hear in the word *happy*?" /ē/.

Build the word *happy*, using the red y tile. h a p p y

"The most common way to spell the sound of /ē/ at the end of a multisyllable word is with a y."

"I will dictate some words. Your job is to clap out the syllables, and **spell one syllable at a time** with the tiles. When you hear the sound of /ē/ at the end of the word, use the letter y."

Dictate the following words:

ugly   **pony**   **bony**   **lady**

If your student uses the blue y letter tile, remind him that blue tiles are consonants and red tiles are vowels. The /ē/ sound is a vowel sound, so we use the red y.

Tip!

Teach Key Card 11: Doubling the Consonant When a Word Ends in /ē/

"Let's go back to the word *happy*." Build the word.

h a p p y

"Divide this word into syllables." *Student divides word.*

h a p   p y

"Read this word, one syllable at a time." *Student responds, "Hap—py."*

"Now say the word fast like we normally say it." *Hă—py.*

Step 8: Y Can Say /ē/

New Teaching
(continued)

"When we say the word, the sound of the first p̠ disappears. *Hă—py*. We don't hear it, but when we spell the word, we put in the p̠. **We double the consonant to protect the short vowel.**"

Remove one of the p̠ tiles.   [h] [a]   [p] [y]

"What would this word say if we only included one p̠?" *Hā—py*.

"We often double the consonant to protect the short vowel." Replace the p̠ in the word *happy*.

Read Key Card 11 with your student and place behind the Review divider.

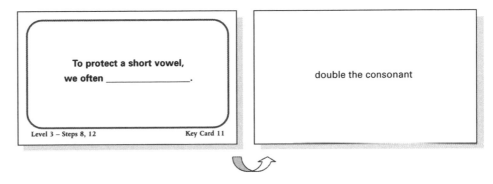

Dictate the following words to your student so he can practice this concept:

penny   bunny   muddy   skinny

"You just learned that we often *double the consonant to protect the short vowel*. But there are some words that do **not** follow this pattern."

Build the word *city*.   [c] [i] [t] [y]

"In the word *city*, we do not double the consonant."

New Teaching
(continued)

Word Cards 41-50: Spell on Paper

Dictate the words and have your student spell them on paper.

41. tiny
42. baby
43. windy
44. city
45. army
46. penny
47. candy
48. forty
49. fifty
50. sixty

Place Word Cards 41-50 behind the Review divider.

If your student tries to spell the sound of final /ē/ with the letter e, take out the Silent E Book.

See all of the reasons for e at the end of a word? E is so busy that we can't use it to make the sound of /ē/ at the end of a multisyllable word. The letter y fills in!

Reinforcement

More Words

Amy	body	bony	copy
grassy	happy	hilly	lady
lazy	lucky	party	pony
puppy	ugly		

Step 8: Y Can Say /ē/

Reinforcement

(continued)

Dictate Sentences

Dictate several sentences each day.

I got this candy for a penny.

Amy was lazy all day!

Sixty kids went to the party.

That lady is in the army.

Are you happy with the pony?

I ate forty clams!

The city is dark and ugly.

The baby is so tiny!

Her puppy has a bony body.

He gave Amy fifty roses.

It is windy on the hilltop.

Dan made a copy of the page.

 How is the daily review going? Are the decks behind the Mastered dividers getting bigger?

Mastered cards will be reviewed in Step 10 to keep them fresh in your student's mind.

Step 9 – Vowel Teams OA and OW

In this lesson your student will learn two more ways to spell the sound of /ō/: oa and ow.

You will need: Word Bank for OA/OW, Word Cards 51-60

Review

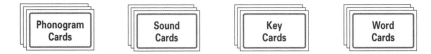

Word Analysis

p o n y   "Divide this word into syllables." *Student divides the word after the o.*

"Read this word." *Pony.*

"Why is the o long?" *It is in an open syllable.*

"What is the last sound you hear in the word *pony*?" /ē/.

"How do we usually spell /ē/ at the end of a word?" *With a y.*

"Label the syllables." *Student uses **Open** tags over both syllables.*

New Teaching

Teach Two More Ways to Spell /ō/

Build the words *open* and *home*.   o p e n   h o m e

"You have learned several ways to spell the sound of /ō/. Let's look at two of the ways."

Divide the word *open* into syllables.   o   p e n

"Why is the o long in the word *open*?" *Because it is at the end of a syllable.*

"Good. The first way to spell the sound of /ō/ is to put it in an open syllable."

New Teaching
(continued)

Point to the word *home*. "Why is the o long in *home?*" *Because of the silent e.*

"Right. The second way to spell the sound of /ō/ is to add a silent e."

"You have also learned two other phonograms that make the sound of /ō/. Pull down those tiles." *Student pulls down the oa and ow tiles.*

"Today we will work on spelling words with the sound of /ō/ spelled oa and ow."

"Which of these tiles can be used at the end of a word?" *Ow.*

"Good. When you hear the sound of /ō/ at the **end** of a word, it is often spelled ow, as in the word *snow.*"

"Change *snow* to *grow.*" *Student changes tiles to spell* grow.

Have your student spell these words with tiles:

slow   **low**   **blow**   **window**

"Some words use the ow tile in the middle of the word, too. Here is an example."

Build the word *own.*

Point to the oa tile. "This tile is used to spell the sound of /ō/ only in the **middle** of a word."

Build the word *boat.*

Point to the oa tile. "Oa is used to spell the /ō/ sound in the word *boat.* It is also used to spell the sound of /ō/ in these next words."

Have your student spell these words with tiles:

goat   **float**   **soap**   **soak**   **oak**

New Teaching
(continued)

Label Syllable Types

Set out the syllable tags. Build the word *toast*. | t | oa | s | t |

"What type of syllable is this word?" *Vowel team syllable, because oa is a vowel team.*

Build the following words. Have your student divide the words into syllables and label each syllable with the proper tag.

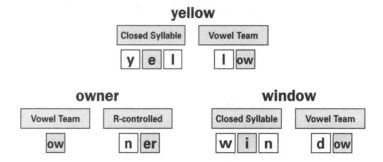

yellow

| Closed Syllable | Vowel Team |
| y | e | l | | l | ow |

owner

| Vowel Team | R-controlled |
| ow | | n | er |

window

| Closed Syllable | Vowel Team |
| w | i | n | | d | ow |

Introduce the Word Bank for OA/OW

Have your student read through the **Word Bank for OA/OW** to improve visual memory. There are several ways to spell the sound of /ō/ and we want students to become very familiar with the words in this Word Bank. This will enable the student to choose the correct spelling of long o when he needs to spell one of these words.

Word Cards 51-60: Spell on Paper

Dictate the words and have your student spell them on paper.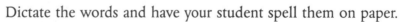

51. snow
52. coat
53. road   The road is slippery.
54. own
55. window
56. yellow
57. boat
58. show
59. grow
60. soap

Place Word Cards 51-60 behind the Review divider.

Reinforcement

More Words

blow	crow	float	foam	glow
goat	load	loan	low	oak
soak	slow	throw	toad	toast

Dictate Sentences

Dictate several sentences each day.

That boy loves the snow!

I blow the foam off my milk.

Do you own a boat?

The oak tree is slow to grow.

A goat ate my toast!

Did Sam throw the soap?

A black crow sat in my window.

I saw a yellow toad by the road.

Will you loan me a coat?

The sky will glow if the sun is low.

Show me how to float on the water.

Dad must soak that load of dishes.

Step 9: Vowel Teams OA and OW

Step 10 – Ways to Spell /ō/

In this lesson, your student will analyze four ways to spell the sound of /ō/.

You will need: Sound Card 49

Review

 Phonogram Cards   Sound Cards   Key Cards   Word Cards

Word Bank for UR
Word Bank for OA/OW

 Quickly review the cards behind the Mastered dividers.

Word Analysis

 **b** i **l** **l** **f** o **l** **d**

"What is a compound word?" *Two smaller words put together.*

"How do you divide compound words?" *Between the two words.*

"Divide this word into syllables." *Student divides.*

"Why are there two l's?" *L's are often doubled after a single vowel in a one-syllable word.*

"What other letters are often doubled?" *F and s.*

"What sound does the i make in this word?" */ĭ/.*

"What sound does o make?" */ō/.*

"Why is the o long?" *O can be long before two consonants.*

Introduce the Word Sort for /ō/ Chart

Write these four headings across the top of lined paper. Draw vertical lines to form four columns:

<u>o</u>	<u>o</u>–<u>e</u>	<u>oa</u>	<u>ow</u>

Point to the column headings. "Here are four ways to spell the sound of /ō/."

Give your student a new sheet of lined paper. "I will dictate a word, and you will write it down on your paper. When you are satisfied that you have spelled the word correctly, copy the word to the correct column on this chart."

Dictate these words:

open	most	vote	show	hose
window	boat	toad	told	hope
over				

Teach Sound Card 49

"Today we have a new Sound Card."

Read Sound Card 49:

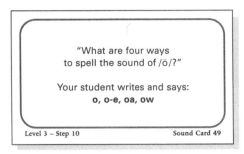

"What are four ways
to spell the sound of /ō/?"

Your student writes and says:
o, o-e, oa, ow

Level 3 – Step 10   Sound Card 49

"Write and say the four ways like this." Say the name of the letters as you write them down: "<u>o</u>, <u>o</u>-consonant-<u>e</u>, <u>oa</u>, <u>ow</u>." Remind your student that we write a *dash* for the word *consonant*.

Practice this Sound Card with your student, and then store it behind the Review divider.

New Teaching
(continued)

More spellings of long o include:

- oe as in *hoe*
- ou as in *boulder*
- ough as in *although*

These spellings aren't used in nearly as many words as the four we studied today and will be covered at a later time.

Reinforcement

Dictate Sentences

Dictate several sentences each day.

Hold the rope for a moment!

I told my robot to put on a coat.

Did you open the hotel window?

I roll down the hill in the snow.

His old boat is made of oak.

Both of us have gold coins.

Do you hope to own a home?

Throw the toast to the crow.

My dog hid the bone in a hole.

Most kids enjoy soap bubbles.

Why did Beth float in the cold water?

Show me how to fold the dress.

Step 11 – Consonant Suffixes

In this lesson, your student will learn three new phonograms and how to spell words containing consonant suffixes.

You will need: letter tiles oo, ea, and ed, Phonogram Cards 48-50, Sound Cards 50-52, Key Card 12, suffix tiles, yellow pencil, jail, Word Cards 61-70

Review

Word Analysis

th o s e   "Read this word."   *Those.*

"What is the first sound you hear?"   /~~th~~/.

"What are the two sounds th can say in a word?" /th/–/~~th~~/.

"What is the second sound in this word?"   /ō/.

"What makes the o long?"   *The silent e.*

"What is the third sound you hear?"   /z/.

"What is the most common way to spell the sound of /z/?"   S.

"Label the syllable."   *Student uses the VCE tag.*

New Teaching

Teach New Phonograms OO, EA, and ED

"We have three new tiles today."

Point to the oo tile.   oo

"This tile says /ōō/–/ŏŏ/–/ō/. Repeat after me: /ōō/–/ŏŏ/–/ō/." *Student repeats.*

New Teaching
(continued)

Point to the ea tile. `ea`

"This tile says /ē/–/ĕ/–/ā/. Repeat after me: /ē/–/ĕ/–/ā/." *Student repeats.*

Point to the ed tile. `ed`

"This tile says /ed/–/d/–/t/. Repeat after me: /ed/–/d/–/t/." *Student repeats.*

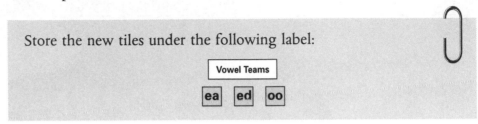

Store the new tiles under the following label:

Vowel Teams

`ea` `ed` `oo`

Take out Phonogram Cards 48, 49, and 50 and practice them with your student.

Practice Sound Cards 50, 51, and 52 with your student. Dictate the sound and have your student write the phonogram.

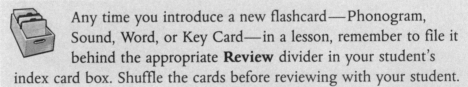

Any time you introduce a new flashcard—Phonogram, Sound, Word, or Key Card—in a lesson, remember to file it behind the appropriate **Review** divider in your student's index card box. Shuffle the cards before reviewing with your student.

If your student doesn't hesitate on a flashcard during the daily review, that card is ready to be filed behind the appropriate **Mastered** divider.

Teach Key Card 12: Suffixes

Build the word *cups*.

"You already know how to make a word plural by adding an s. The s is called a **suffix**. A **suffix** is a word ending. It can be added to a **base word** to make a new word."

Build the suffix *ful*. `f` `u` `l`

Step 11: Consonant Suffixes

New Teaching
(continued)

"Today you are going to learn more suffixes. The suffix *ful* is one example. We can add *ful* to the word *cup*."

"What does this word say?" *Cupful.*

"*Cup* is called the **base word**, and *ful* is the **suffix**."

Build the suffix *ness*. `n` `e` `s` `s`

"Here is another suffix. We can add it to the word *glad* to make a new word."

`g` `l` `a` `d` `n` `e` `s` `s`

"What does this word say?" *Gladness.*

"What is the base word?" *Glad.*

Read Key Card 12 with your student and place behind the Review divider.

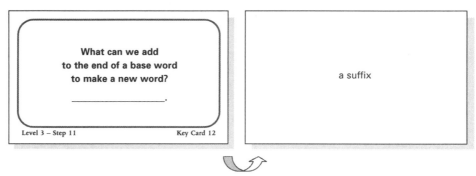

Sort Consonant Suffixes and Vowel Suffixes

Place the suffix tiles on the table. "These are all suffixes. Some begin with consonants, and some begin with vowels. Let's sort them into two piles."

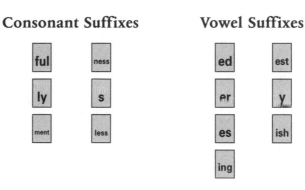

Consonant Suffixes		Vowel Suffixes	
ful	ness	ed	est
ly	s	er	y
ment	less	es	ish
		ing	

Teach Words with Consonant Suffixes

"Today we are only going to work with the consonant suffixes." Put away the vowel suffixes.

"I am going to dictate some words. First spell the base word with tiles, then add the consonant suffix tile."

quickly	**sadness**	**shipment**	**helpful**
candles	**pavement**	**illness**	**careful**
careless			

Teach *Lone, Only,* and Rule Breakers *One* and *Once*

Build the word *lone*. | l | o | n | e |

"The word *lone* means 'by itself.' There is just one, as in *a lone wolf*."

Cover up the l in the word *lone*.

"The word *one* is hidden inside the word *lone*."

Take out Word Card 68. "The word *one* doesn't follow the rules. It is a Rule Breaker. We hear the sound /w/ in the word *one*, but we don't spell it with a w. Circle the o in this word." Have your student fill in the circle with yellow pencil and throw the Word Card in jail.

"Spell the word *one*." *Student spells the word.*

"Here is a related word." Build the word *once*. | o | n | c | e |

"The word *once* has a silent e. What is the job of silent e in this word?" *To make the c soft.*

Take out Word Card 69. "The word *once* is another Rule Breaker. Why?" *Because we hear the sound /w/ but don't spell it with a w.*

"Circle and color the o and throw this word in jail."

"Spell the word *once*." *Student spells the word.*

Build the word *only*. | o | n | l | y |

"Point to the vowels in the word *only*, and tell me what sound they each make." *Student points to the o and says /ō/. Student points to the y and says /ē/.*

"This word does follow the rules. Spell the word *only*." *Student spells the word.*

Practice these four words until they become easy for your student.

Silent E Book: Identify the Job of Silent E

Have your student enter these words on the correct page of his Silent E Book:

grace (pgs. 1 and/or 2)   **use** (pg. 1)   **one** (pg. 5)
once (pg. 2)   **puzzle** (pg. 4)

Word Cards 61-70: Spell with Tiles

To give your student more practice with recognizing and adding suffixes, first have him spell the words using the letter tiles and suffix tiles.

61. thankful

62. silently

63. cheerful

64. spotless

65. gladly

66. darkness

67. graceful

68. one   You can have one cookie.

69. once

70. only

> Note that when *ful* is used as a suffix, it only has one l̲. A common problem is to add two l's.

Spell on Paper

Once your student is able to spell the words using the tiles, dictate Word Cards 61-70 and have him spell the words on paper.

Place Word Cards 61-70 behind the Review divider.

Reinforcement
(continued)

More Words

blindness	boldly	coats	coldness
cupful	cuteness	days	fitness
forgetful	forgiveness	gladness	hardness
harmful	helpful	hurtful	illness
kindness	loudness	mindful	moistness
mouthful	pavement	placement	priceless
ripeness	roads	sadness	scrapes
sharpness	shipment	stands	stiffness
thickness	useful		

Dictate Sentences

Dictate several sentences each day.

I enjoy the coldness of winter.
Once I went to bed gladly and silently.
Mom was thankful for my kindness!
The cuteness of the puppy made me cheerful.
Bob stands still in the darkness.
I ate a mouthful of grapes.
We have one box of priceless dishes.
The shipment of coats is here.
My fish swims boldly in a cupful of water.
Sue is swift and graceful as she swims.
Moistness on the roads can be harmful.
Will you ask for her forgiveness?

Step 11: Consonant Suffixes

In this lesson, your student will learn how to spell words containing vowel suffixes.

You will need: Key Card 11 (taught in Step 8), Word Cards 71-80

Review

Word Bank for AI/AY
Word Bank for OA/OW

Word Analysis

"How many syllables do you hear in the word *forgetful?*" *Three.*

"What is the suffix in this word?" *Ful.*

"Divide the word so the suffix is in its own syllable." *Student divides the word before the suffix.*

"What is the base word?" *Forget.*

"Divide the base word into syllables." *Student divides before the g.*

"Label the syllables." *Student uses **R-controlled**, **Closed**, and **Closed** tags.*

New Teaching

Apply Key Card 11: Doubling the Consonant When Adding a Vowel Suffix

Take out the consonant and vowel suffixes. Have your student sort the suffixes into two piles: consonant suffixes and vowel suffixes. Set aside suffix ed for now—it will be covered in Step 19.

"Today we are only going to work with the vowel suffixes." Put away the consonant suffixes.

"Vowel suffixes are very friendly. They like to take the consonant before them and run off to play. I'll show you what I mean."

Build the word *tap*.   t | a | p

"I want to make the word *tap* into *tapping*."

"When I add suffix <u>ing</u> to the word *tap*, like this...   t | a | p | ing

...the friendly vowel suffix grabs on to the p and runs off."

"When the vowel suffix runs off with the p, the <u>a</u> is left open." Point to the <u>a</u>. "Now the <u>a</u> is long. What does this word say?" *Taping.*

"Right. That isn't the word we want, is it? We need to protect the short vowel by closing the syllable. We add an extra p."

t | a | p   p | ing

"Now read the word." *Student reads* tapping.

"Much better. So you can see that sometimes we have to **protect the short vowel** by doubling the consonant."

Read Key Card 11 with your student and file behind the Review divider.

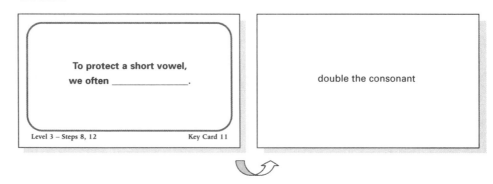

Teach More about Adding Vowel Suffixes

Build the word *wet*.   w | e | t

"Add friendly vowel suffix <u>er</u> to form the word *wetter*." *Student doubles the t and adds suffix <u>er</u>.*

New Teaching
(continued)

If your student needs extra work with this concept, have him practice with these words:

stop - stopping
plan - planning
swim - swimming

Demonstrate the "friendly vowel suffix" running off with the last consonant in the word. Show that it is necessary to close the syllable to protect the short vowel.

"Sometimes the friendly vowel suffix runs off with the last consonant and we **don't** have to protect the vowel – it is already protected. Look at the word *darker*."

| d | ar | k | er |

"The friendly vowel suffix runs off with the last consonant."

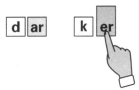

"There is no short vowel that needs protection, so we don't double the consonant."

Demonstrate this concept with these words:

printing   **coldest**   **faster**   **oily**

Word Cards 71-80: Spell with Tiles

To give your student more practice with recognizing and adding suffixes, first have him spell the words using the letter and suffix tiles.

71. running
72. printing
73. loudest
74. stopping
75. helper
76. planning
77. standing
78. crispy
79. swimmer
80. wetter

New Teaching
(continued)

Spell on Paper

Once your student is able to spell the words using the tiles, dictate Word Cards 71-80 and have him spell the words on paper.

Place Word Cards 71-80 behind the Review divider.

Reinforcement

More Words

camping	childish	chopping	coldest
cutting	darker	ending	fastest
handy	helping	inches	jogger
mopping	napping	oily	oldest
riches	rotting	sandy	strongest
thickest			

Dictate Sentences

Dictate several sentences each day.

Why are you chopping down the tree?

We will go camping in August.

My helper is mopping up the water.

Do you want to go running?

The jogger is standing still now.

The baby is napping.

I am helping Sue make crispy shrimp.

I think the ending of the song is sad.

Ken is planning a big party.

That swimmer is wetter than a fish!

A green apple is rotting on the table.

Mom is so handy at home!

Step 12: Vowel Suffixes

Step 13 – The 1-1-1 Rule

This lesson will teach the 1-1-1 Rule for adding suffixes.

You will need: Key Cards 13 and 14, 1-1-1 Rule Chart, Word Cards 81-90

Review

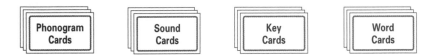

Word Bank for UR

Word Analysis

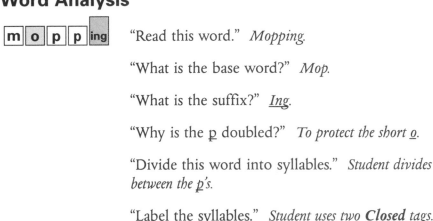

"Read this word." *Mopping.*

"What is the base word?" *Mop.*

"What is the suffix?" *Ing.*

"Why is the p doubled?" *To protect the short o.*

"Divide this word into syllables." *Student divides between the p's.*

"Label the syllables." *Student uses two* **Closed** *tags.*

New Teaching

Teach Key Card 13: Demonstrate the Difference between Adding Consonant Suffixes and Vowel Suffixes

With your student, sort the suffixes into two piles: consonant suffixes and vowel suffixes.

Keep the consonant suffixes in front of your student and set aside the vowel suffixes. Point to the consonant suffixes. "Adding a **consonant** suffix to a base word is easy."

Build the word *hope.* "Choose one of the consonant suffixes and add it to the word *hope.*" *Student makes the word* hopeless *or* hopeful.

"Correct. To spell this word, you just add the consonant suffix. You do not change the base word."

Set aside the consonant suffixes. Put the vowel suffixes in front of your student.

"**Vowel** suffixes are different, aren't they? When we add a **vowel** suffix, sometimes we need to **double** the last consonant of the base word and sometimes we don't."

"Let's spell the word *hunting*." | h | u | n | t |ing|

Show the friendly vowel suffix grabbing the t and running off with it. Your student will see that the short u is already protected, and the final consonant does not need to be doubled.

Read Key Card 13 with your student and place behind the Review divider.

1. When we add a *consonant* suffix, do we double the last consonant of the base word? _____ .		1. no
2. When we add a *vowel* suffix, do we double the last consonant of the base word? _____ .		2. sometimes
Level 3 – Step 13 Key Card 13		

Teach Key Card 14: The 1-1-1 Rule

The idea of the "friendly vowel suffix" was used as a transition to help your student understand why the consonant is doubled at the end of some words before adding a suffix. Next, your student will learn the 1-1-1 Rule, which will expand his understanding of this concept.

"Let's take a close look at the word *win*." | w | i | n |

"How many **syllables** are in the word *win*?" *One.*

"How many **vowels** are there?" *One.*

"How many **consonants** at the end?" *One.*

New Teaching
(continued)

"When the answer to **all** of these questions is *one*, **double** the consonant before adding a vowel suffix."

Take out the 1-1-1 Rule Chart.

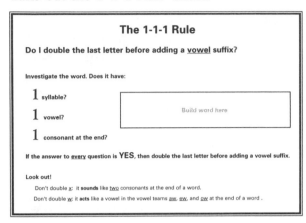

Using the steps on the 1-1-1 Rule Chart, investigate the following words to see if the final consonant needs to be doubled. Build the words in the box provided and encourage your student to use his detective skills..

bed + **ing**	Yes, double the <u>d</u>.
can + **ing**	Yes, double the <u>n</u>.
glad + **ly**	No, we don't double the <u>d</u>. The 1-1-1 Rule only applies to **vowel** suffixes.
jump + **ing**	No, there are two consonants at the end of the base word, not just one.
map + **ing**	Yes, double the <u>p</u>.
help + **er**	No, there are two consonants at the end of the base word, not just one.
win + **ing**	Yes, double the <u>n</u>.
do + **ing**	No, there is no consonant at the end of the base word.
sip + **ing**	Yes, double the <u>p</u>.
stir + **ing**	Yes. Even though <u>ir</u> comes together on a tile, the <u>r</u> is still a consonant, so double the <u>r</u>.
sail + **ing**	No, there are two vowels, not just one.
blur + **y**	Yes, double the <u>r</u>.

snow + ing	No, there is no consonant sound at the end. The <u>w</u> is acting like a vowel when it is in the vowel team <u>ow</u>.
sleep + y	No, there are two vowels, not just one.
start + ing	No, there are two consonants at the end of the base word, not just one.
win + er	Yes, double the <u>n</u>.
shop + ing	Yes, double the <u>p</u>.
fish + ing	No, there are two consonants at the end of the base word, not just one.
thaw + ing	No, there is no consonant sound at the end. The <u>w</u> is acting like a vowel when it is in a vowel team.

Read Key Card 14 with your student and place behind the Review divider.

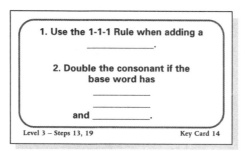

1. Use the 1-1-1 Rule when adding a
   _____.

2. Double the consonant if the base word has

   _____
   _____

   and _____.

Level 3 – Steps 13, 19   Key Card 14

1. vowel suffix

2. <u>1</u> syllable
   <u>1</u> vowel
   <u>1</u> consonant at the end

Explain That X Is Not Doubled

Pull down the letter tile <u>x</u>. | x |

"Tell me the sound of this tile." /*ks*/.

"There are two sounds, /k/ and /s/, and we say them quickly together."

Build the word *box*.

"When we add a vowel suffix to the word *box*, we don't double the <u>x</u>. It already sounds like two consonants, so we don't need to double it."

Have your student spell these words:

fixing   **foxes**   **taxes**

Word Cards 81-90: Spell on Paper

Starting again with this lesson, have your student spell the words
immediately on paper. If he has difficulty with a word, let him
spell it first with the letter and suffix tiles.

81. parking
82. waiting
83. drawing
84. runner
85. boxes
86. muddy
87. slower
88. owner
89. digging
90. keeping

Place Word Cards 81-90 behind the Review divider.

Reinforcement

More Words

bedding	doing	fishing	jumping
sailing	shopping	sipping	skipping
snowing	thawing	winner	winning

Dictate Sentences

Dictate several sentences each day.

Pam is gladly doing the shopping.
That runner is slower than a snail!
Why are you jumping and skipping?
The ice on the road is thawing now.
We go fishing and sailing in June.
Bob is winning the race.
The winner is keeping all the candy.
The owner of the pony is waiting for me.
I saw my face in the muddy puddle.
Sam is digging a hole in the clay.
Amy is sipping her drink.
My helper put the bedding in the boxes.

Step 14 – Words Beginning with WH

In this lesson, your student will learn words beginning with wh and the six question words: who, what, where, when, why, and how.

You will need: Key Card 15, yellow pencil, jail, Word Cards 91-100

Review

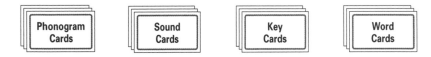

Word Analysis

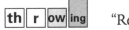

"Read this word." *Throwing.*

"What is the base word?" *Throw.*

"What is the suffix?" *Ing.*

"Is it a vowel suffix or a consonant suffix?" *Vowel suffix.*

"What letters make up the /ō/ sound?" *Ow.*

"Divide this word into syllables." *Student divides before the i.*

"Label the syllables." *Student uses the **Vowel Team** and **Closed** tags.*

New Teaching

Teach Key Card 15: The Six Question Words

"There are six words that newspaper reporters use when they write an article: *who, what, where, when, why,* and *how.* We call these the **six question words**. Repeat them after me: *who, what, where, when, why,* and *how.*" *Student repeats.*

Show the back of Key Card 15 to your student.

New Teaching
(continued)

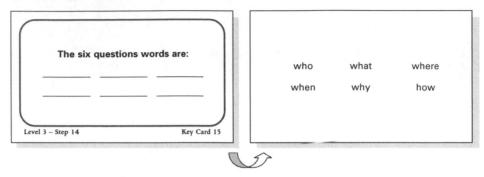

"Here are the six question words. Read them." *Who, what, where, when, why* and *how.*

"Notice that five of these words begin with wh."

Once your student has a good grasp on the question words, file the Key Card behind the Review divider.

The six questions words are:

_____ _____ _____

_____ _____ _____

Level 3 – Step 14   Key Card 15

| who | what | where |
| when | why | how |

> **Tip!** Note that the student is not spelling these words at this point; he is only learning what the six question words are. He will spell them in the next activity.

In many areas, the /hw/ sound has been lost. The words *what* and *when* are commonly misspelled by beginners who don't hear the extra breath of the wh.

If your student has a difficult time distinguishing between the /w/ of w and the /hw/ of wh in spoken words, knowing the question words can prevent misspellings.

Teach Three Rule Breakers

"Some of the question words are Rule Breakers. Let's find out which ones they are."

Take out Word Card 92. "*What* is a Rule Breaker. Which letter doesn't make the sound we expect it to?" *The a sounds like /ŭ/.*

"Right. Circle the a and color it yellow. What do we do with Rule Breakers?" *Throw them in jail.*

"Spell the word *what* on paper." *Student writes the word.*

Take out Word Card 91. "*Who* is another Rule Breaker. Can you figure out why?" *The wh doesn't say /hw/. It says /h/.*

"Circle the wh, since it doesn't make the sound we expect it to." *Student circles the wh in yellow.*

"Throw the Rule Breaker in jail." *Student puts Word Card 91 behind bars.*

Step 14: Words Beginning with WH

New Teaching
(continued)

"Spell the word *who* on paper." *Student writes the word.*

Build the word *who* with tiles. `wh` `o`

"We can change *who* to *whose* by adding *se*." `wh` `o` `s` `e`

"*Whose,* as in *whose pencil is this?*"

Take out Word Card 100. "*Whose* is a Rule Breaker. Which letters don't make the sound we expect them to make?" *Wh*.

Have your student circle the <u>wh</u> and put Word Card 100 in jail.

"Spell the word *whose* on paper." *Student writes the word.*

Have your student practice these three words until they become easy.

Teach the Word *Where*

"Spell the word *here* with tiles. *Here,* as in *Come here.*" *Student spells the word.*

`h` `e` `r` `e`

"We can change the word *here* to *where*."

Replace the <u>h</u> tile with the <u>wh</u> tile. `wh` `e` `r` `e`

"*Where,* as in *where are you?*"

> If the word *where* gives your student any trouble, you can put it in jail. The <u>e</u> is usually considered a short <u>e</u>, but in the normal rhythm of speech, the <u>r</u> distorts the vowel sound. In many regions the vowel sound "slides" from /ĕ/ to /ā/. **Tip!**
>
> You can either tell your student to "pronounce for spelling" or treat the word like a Rule Breaker.

Silent E Book: Identify the Job of Silent E

Have your student enter these words on the correct page of his Silent E Book:

whale (pg. 1)	**whose** (pg. 5)	**white** (pg. 1)
gentle (pg. 4)	**where** (pg. 5)	

New Teaching
(continued)

Practice Additional Words Containing WH

Take out Word Cards 91-100. "Let's read through each of these words. As you read them, listen for the /hw/ sound at the beginning."

As you read each word together, have your student hold his hand up in front of his mouth to feel his breath. If he normally doesn't use the sound /hw/, tell him to "pronounce for spelling."

Have your student build the following words with letter tiles:

white   **which**   **whisper**   **wheel**   **whale**

Word Cards 91-100: Spell on Paper

Dictate the words and have your student spell them on paper.

91. who

92. what

93. where   Where is your sister?

94. when

95. white

96. which   Which one do you like best?

97. whisper

98. wheel   The wheel on my bike is flat.

99. whale   I saw a whale in the ocean.

100. whose

Place Word Cards 91-100 behind the Review divider.

Reinforcement

Dictate Sentences

Dictate several sentences each day.

Who is napping on the bed?

What song do you like most?

Where can I put this little pig?

When will you return home?

A crow is on the white fence.

Which puppy do you want?

Whisper when you are in class.

The wheel of my bike is broken.

Did you see the whale jumping?

Whose toad is on the table?

Which white sheep is running?

Who or what is digging up the flowers?

Writing Station

In this new lesson section, dictate the words and have your student say and write the base word, and then add the suffix. Next have your student create original sentences using the new words. Encourage him to see the relation between the words and to use his imagination!

rainy   **dripping**   **ponds**   **melting**   **quickly**

New! Up until this point, your student has been writing words and sentences from dictation. Now it is time to give your student more opportunities to USE his spelling skills. The Writing Station does just that. You will note that the words here are related for added interest and to encourage your student to combine his imagination and spelling skills to create original sentences.

Many students can spell words correctly in class but have difficulty in practical situations. Exercises like the Writing Station provide the practice and structure your student needs to achieve the goal of correct spelling outside the classroom.

Your student is halfway there! Has he been filling out his Progress Chart?

Step 15 – The Sound of /o͞o/ Spelled OO

In this lesson, your student will learn to spell words containing the sound of /o͞o/ spelled oo.

You will need: Homophones List, yellow pencil, jail, Word Cards 101-110

Review

Word Bank for OA/OW

Word Analysis

| h | i | n | g | e |

"Read this word." *Hinge.*

"What is the last sound you hear in the word *hinge?*" */j/.*

"Why can't we spell /j/ with the letter j?" *English words don't end in j.*

"How do we spell the /j/ sound in this word?" *G (or ge).*

"What is the job of the silent e?" *To make the g soft.*

New Teaching

Teach Another Way to Spell /o͞o/

Build the words *do* and *student*.

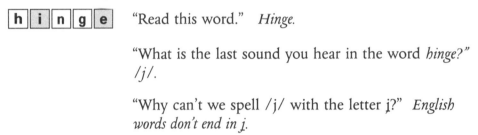

"You have learned several ways to spell the sound of /o͞o/. Point to the tiles that say the sound of /o͞o/ in these words." *Student points to the o tile in the word* do *and the u tile in the word* student.

"Right. You have also learned another phonogram that makes the sound of /o͞o/. Pull down that tile." *Student pulls down the oo tile.*

New Teaching

(continued)

"Today we will work on spelling words with the sound of /o͞o/ spelled oo."

Build the word *food*. ⬛ f oo d

Point to the oo tile. "What sound does this tile make in the word *food?*" /o͞o/.

"Using this tile, spell the word *tool*." *Student spells the word with tiles.*

"I will change it to *school*." ⬛ s ch oo l

Point to the ch tile. "What sound does the ch tile make in the word *school?*" /k/.

"Good. I will dictate some words. The /o͞o/ sound in these words is spelled with the oo tile."

Dictate the following words:

room   noon   cool

Homophones List: Add the Words *To* and *Too*

Build the word *too*. t oo

"Read this word." *Too.*

"*Too,* as in *I'd like to go, too.* In this sentence, *too* means *also.*"

"We can also say, *The boat weighs too much.* In this sentence, *too* means *more than enough.*"

"Write *to* and *too* on your Homophones List." *Student writes the words.*

Read the following sentences. Student should point to the correct word on the Homophones List.

Jacob laughed <u>too</u> hard.
Would you like some milk, <u>too</u>?
Let's go <u>to</u> the park.
I like <u>to</u> water ski.

Teach Two Rule Breakers

Build the word *many*.

"The word *many* is a Rule Breaker. Which letter doesn't say the sound we expect it to say?" *The letter a.*

Take out Word Card 109. "What do we do with Rule Breakers?" *Student circles the a, colors in the circle with yellow pencil, and throws the Word Card in jail.*

"Write the word *many*." *Student writes the word.*

"If we take away the m, what word are we left with?" *Any.*

Take out Word Card 110. "*Any* is another Rule Breaker. Which letter should you circle and color in?" *The a.*

Have the student throw the Rule Breaker in jail.

"Write the word *any*." *Student writes the word.*

Word Cards 101-110: Spell on Paper

Dictate the words and have your student spell them on paper.

101. tooth
102. school
103. room
104. soon
105. too   Your sister can come, too.
106. food
107. spoon
108. noon
109. many
110. any

> In each of these words, the sound of /o͞o/ is spelled <u>oo</u>. **Tip!**

Place Word Cards 101-110 behind the Review divider.

Reinforcement

Dictate Sentences

Dictate several sentences each day.

I lost a tooth at school today.

Mom told me to go to my room.

Do you like the food at school?

Amy stuck a spoon in the jam jar.

I have too many lazy ducks!

Will you ride your bike at noon?

I hope we go camping soon.

I do not giggle too much!

Do you have any older sisters?

I am thankful for my spotless room.

That man has a gold tooth!

Do you want any food now?

Writing Station

Dictate each word. Have your student say and write the base word, add the suffix, and write original sentences using the new words.

feeding   spoonful   toothless   sobbing   plays

Step 15: The Sound of /o͞o/ Spelled OO

Step 16 – Ways to Spell /k/

In this lesson, your student will analyze four ways to spell the sound of /k/.

You will need: Sound Card 53

Review

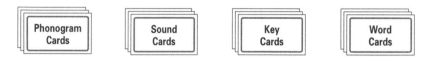

Word Bank for AI/AY

Word Analysis

l u ck y   "Read this word." *Lucky.*

"What is the base word?" *Luck.*

"What is the suffix?" *Y (or /ē/).*

"Is the y a vowel or consonant in this word?" *Vowel.*

"What spells the sound of /k/ in this word?" *Ck.*

"Why can we use ck?" *We can use ck after a short vowel.*

"Divide this word into syllables." *Student divides before the y.*

"Label the syllable types." *Student uses the **Closed** and **Open** tags.*

New Teaching

Introduce the Word Sort for /k/ Chart

Write these four headings across the top of lined paper. Draw vertical lines to form four columns:

c	k	ck	ch

Point to the column headings. "Here are four ways to spell the sound of /k/."

New Teaching
(continued)

Give your student a new sheet of lined paper. "I will dictate a word, and you will write it down on your paper. When you are satisfied that you have spelled the word correctly, copy the word to the correct column on this chart."

Dictate these words:

thick	**school**	**oink**	**scalp**
lake	**broke**	**cabin**	**think**
sock	**rake**		

Teach Sound Card 53

"Today we have a new Sound Card."

Read Sound Card 53:

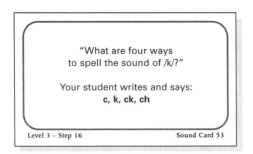

"Write and say the four ways like this." Say the name of the letters as you write them down: "c, k, ck, ch."

Practice this Sound Card with your student, and then store it behind the Review divider.

Step 16: Ways to Spell /k/

Dictate Sentences

Dictate several sentences each day.

> **A bobcat is napping on that cliff.**
>
> **Did Mike just quack like a duck?**
>
> **Who will kiss me on the cheek?**
>
> **Have fun at the ice rink!**
>
> **Thank you for the pink kite!**
>
> **Frank ate popcorn at school once.**
>
> **The king and queen ate sweet cakes.**
>
> **Kim is parking her black car.**
>
> **Last week I got a cute backpack.**
>
> **The kind cow stands under the oak tree.**
>
> **Uncle Rick will make crispy catfish.**
>
> **Ask Ken to check the lock on his bike.**

Writing Station

Dictate each word and have your student say and write the base word, add the suffix, and write original sentences using the new words.

sticky   **getting**   **smaller**   **snacking**   **sweetness**

In this lesson, the student will learn to spell words containing the sound of /ē/ spelled ea.

You will need: Word Bank for EA, Homophones List, Word Cards 111-120

Review

Phonogram Cards   Sound Cards   Key Cards   Word Cards

Word Analysis

"Read this word." *Spoils.*

"One s says /s/ and the other says /z/. Which one says /z/?" *The second one.*

"What is the base word?" *Spoil.*

"What is the suffix?" *S.*

"Is it a vowel or consonant suffix?" *Consonant.*

"Label the syllable." *Student uses the **Vowel Team** tag.*

New Teaching

Teach Another Way to Spell /ē/

Build the words *he, Steve, feet,* and *happy.*

"You have learned several ways to spell the sound of /ē/."

"Look at these four words. Point to the vowel team that spells the sound of /ē/." *Student points to the vowel team ee tile in the word* feet.

"Now point to the most common way to spell the sound of /ē/ at the end of a word." *Student points to the y tile in the word* happy.

New Teaching
(continued)

Point to the word *he.* "Why is the <u>e</u> long in the word *he?*" *Because it is in an open syllable.*

Point to the word *Steve.* "Why is the <u>e</u> long in the word *Steve?*" *Because of the silent <u>e</u>.*

"Good. You have also learned another phonogram that makes the sound of /ē/. Pull down that tile." *Student pulls down the <u>ea</u> tile.*

"Today we will work on spelling words with the sound of /ē/ spelled <u>ea</u>."

Build the word *team.* | t || ea || m |

Point to the <u>ea</u> tile. "What sound does this tile have in this word?" /ē/.

"Using this tile, spell the word *read,* as in, *I will read the mail.*" *Student spells the word with tiles.*

"I will dictate some words. The /ē/ sound in these words is spelled with the <u>ea</u> tile."

Dictate the following words:

mean   **speak**   **eat**   **deal**

Introduce the Word Bank for EA

Have your student read through the **Word Bank for EA** to improve visual memory. There are several ways to spell the sound of /ē/ and we want students to become very familiar with the words in this Word Bank. This will enable the student to choose the correct spelling of long <u>e</u> when he needs to spell one of these words.

Homophones List: Add the Words *Here* and *Hear*

Build the word *hear.* | h || ea || r |

"Read this word." *Hear.*

"*Hear,* as in *I can hear you.*"

"Write *here* and *hear* on your Homophones List." *Student writes the words.*

Step 17: Long E Spelled EA

New Teaching
(continued)

Read the following sentences. Student should point to the correct word on the Homophones List.

Would you come over <u>here</u>, please?

Can you <u>hear</u> the music?

Let's stay <u>here</u> today.

Amy did not <u>hear</u> me.

Silent E Book: Identify the Job of Silent E

Spell the word *please* with tiles. | p | l | ea | s | e |

"The word *please* has a silent <u>e</u>."

Take out the Silent E Book. Have your student determine the page on which to enter this word. Help him to see that it belongs on page 5 under Handyman E because the job of silent <u>e</u> doesn't fall under any of the other four categories. *Student enters the word.*

> You may wish to share this explanation with your student:
>
> In words like *please, moose,* and *house,* the silent <u>e</u> is added so the word doesn't look like a plural word *(pleas, moos, hous).*

Teach a High-Frequency Word

Spell the word *from* with the letter tiles. | f | r | o | m |

"What sound does the <u>o</u> have in this word?" /ŭ/.

"Good. When you get to this word, remember that the /ŭ/ sound is spelled with an <u>o</u> in this word."

Word Cards 111-120: Spell on Paper
Dictate the words and have your student spell them on paper.

111. eat
112. please
113. year
114. read   I will read a book.
115. hear   Do you hear a sound?
116. each
117. team   Whose team are you on?
118. clean
119. near
120. from

Place Word Cards 111-120 behind the Review divider.

Reinforcement

More Words

clear	**deal**	**ear**	**lead** (lead the parade)
mean	**reach**	**speak**	**teach**

Dictate Sentences
Dictate several sentences each day.

Did you hear me speak?

A hawk will fly in the clear blue sky.

Please clean your room this year!

Can you reach the stars?

Lead me to your mean king!

Do you live near the school?

Whisper your wish in my ear.

Will you make a deal with me?

Each team will need a ball.

Is your aunt from the city?

Can you eat sixty cakes?

I cannot hear Amy read from here.

Reinforcement
(continued)

Writing Station

Dictate each word. Have your student say and write the base word, add the suffix, and write original sentences using the new words.

petting   **brushes**   **eating**   **sniffs**   **noses**

Step 18 – Ways to Spell /ē/

In this lesson, your student will learn three new phonograms and analyze five ways to spell the sound of /ē/.

You will need: letter tiles igh, ir, and ey, Phonogram Cards 51-53, Sound Cards 54-57

Review

Word Bank for UR

Word Analysis

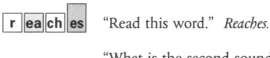
"Read this word." *Reaches.*

"What is the second sound you hear?" /ē/.

"What letters are used to spell the /ē/ sound?" *Ea.*

"What is the base word?" *Reach.*

"What is the suffix?" *Es.*

"Is it a vowel or consonant suffix?" *Vowel.*

"Divide this word into syllables." *Student divides after the ch.*

"Label the syllables." *Student uses the **Vowel Team** and **Closed** tags.*

New Teaching

Teach New Phonograms IGH, IR, and EY

"We have three new tiles today."

Point to the igh tile.   **igh**

"This tile says /ī/, **three-letter /ī/**. Repeat after me: /ī/, **three-letter /ī/**." *Student repeats.*

New Teaching
(continued)

Point to the <u>ir</u> tile. `ir`

"This tile says **/er/ as in** *first.* Repeat after me: **/er/ as in** *first.*"
Student repeats.

Point to the <u>ey</u> tile. `ey`

"This tile says **/ā/–/ē/ that we may use at the end of English words.** Repeat after me: **/ā/–/ē/** that we **may** use at the end of English words." *Student repeats.*

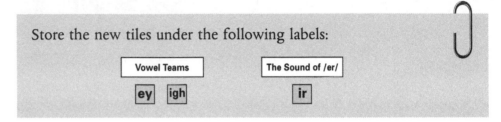

Store the new tiles under the following labels:

Vowel Teams	The Sound of /er/
`ey` `igh`	`ir`

Take out Phonogram Cards 51, 52, and 53 and practice them with your student.

Practice Sound Cards 54, 55, and 56. Dictate the sound and have your student write the phonogram.

Introduce the Word Sort for /ē/ Chart

Write these five headings across the top of lined paper. Draw vertical lines to form five columns:

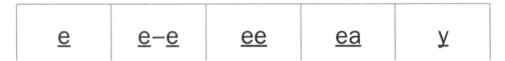

<u>e</u>	<u>e–e</u>	<u>ee</u>	<u>ea</u>	<u>y</u>

Point to the column headings. "Here are five ways to spell the sound of /ē/."

Give your student a new sheet of lined paper. "I will dictate a word, and you will write it down on your paper. When you are satisfied that you have spelled the word correctly, copy the word to the correct column on this chart."

Dictate these words:

even	**hear**	**these**	**eat**
sleep	**sticky**	**tree**	**she**
Steve	**funny**		

New Teaching
(continued)

Teach Sound Card 57

"Today we have a new Sound Card."

Read Sound Card 57:

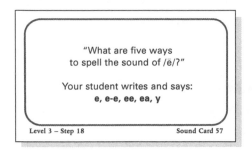

"What are five ways
to spell the sound of /ē/?"

Your student writes and says:
e, e-e, ee, ea, y

Level 3 – Step 18   Sound Card 57

"Write and say the five ways like this." Say the name of the letters as you write them down: "e̲, e̲-consonant-e̲, e̲e̲, e̲a̲, y̲." Remind your student that we write a *dash* for the word *consonant*.

Practice this Sound Card with your student, and then store it behind the Review divider.

More spellings of long e̲ include:
- i̲ as in *machine*
- e̲i̲ as in *seize*
- i̲e̲ as in *field*
- e̲y̲ as in *monkey*

With the exception of i̲, these spellings aren't used in nearly as many words as the five we studied today. They will be covered at a later time.

Dictate Sentences

Dictate several sentences each day.

Even the queen began to eat.

Did you feed the three sheep?

I hear a bee near my ear.

Lead the deer to the tree.

Please let the child sleep.

Do you need a refund?

These fifteen sheets belong to me.

My teeth seem to be green!

We can see the team from here.

The water is deep and clear.

He made a deal with each boy.

She has not seen me for a year.

Writing Station

Dictate each word. Have your student say and write the base word, add the suffix, and write original sentences using the new words.

teacher   reading   papers   smarter   staples

Step 19 – Suffix ED

In this lesson, your student will learn to recognize the three sounds of suffix ed, identify the base word of past tense words, and form past tense words by adding ed.

You will need: Key Card 14 (taught in Step 13), Key Cards 16 and 17, ED Word Sheet, ed suffix tile, Word Cards 121-130

Review

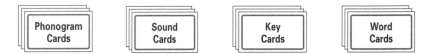

Word Bank for EA

Before the lesson, cut apart the words on the ED Word Sheet.

Word Analysis

<table>
<tr><td>p</td><td>ur</td><td>p</td><td>l</td><td>e</td></tr>
</table>

"Read this word." *Purple.*

"What is the second sound you hear in this word?" */er/.*

"How is /er/ spelled in this word?" *Ur.*

"Do you pronounce the e at the end of this word?" *No.*

"What is the job of the silent e here?" *To add a vowel to the syllable.*

"Divide this word into syllables." *Student counts back three tiles and divides.*

"Label the syllables." *Student uses the **R-controlled** and **C+le** tags.*

Division Rule #4

To divide the syllables in a C+le word, count back three letters and divide.

New Teaching

Teach Key Card 16: The Term *Past Tense*

Build the word *plant*.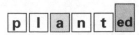

"Today I **plant**. Yesterday I **planted**." Add the suffix tile <u>ed</u> to the word.

p l a n t ed

"When I say that I **planted** yesterday, I am talking about something that happened **in the past**. We say that **planted** is in the **past tense**."

"What did I add to the word *plant* to make the word *planted*, something that happened in the past?" *Student replies* <u>ed</u>.

"Finish this sentence: Today I **bake**. Yesterday I _____." *Baked.*

"Good. Today I **play**. Yesterday I _____." *Played.*

Read Key Card 16 with your student.

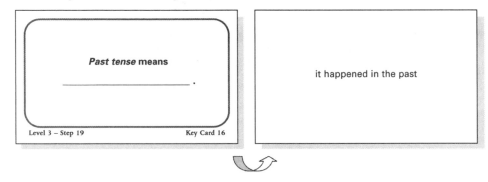

Place the Key Card behind the Review divider.

Introduce ED Sorting Activity

Take out the words from the ED Word Sheet, which you cut apart earlier.

Set out the following words:

| twisted | jogged | stepped |

"You know that <u>ed</u> has three sounds. Tell me the three sounds." *Student replies /ed/–/d/–/t/.*

"In the word *twisted*, which sound does <u>ed</u> make?" *Student replies /ed/.*

"In the word *jogged*, which sound does it make?" */d/.*

"What about in the word *stepped*?" */t/.*

Step 19: Suffix ED

New Teaching
(continued)

Set out the three headings.

| sounds like **ed** | sounds like **d** | sounds like **t** |

"Here are the three different sounds of ed." Read the headings with your student.

"We will sort some words under the correct headings." Use the words that you cut apart earlier.

Walk the student through the first several words.
1. Read the word.
2. Decide which sound ed makes in the word.
3. Put the word under the correct heading.

Teach Key Card 17: Identify Base Words of Past Tense Words

It is important that the student be able to identify the base word when he hears a past tense word. You don't want your student to hear the word *camped*, for instance, and spell it *campt*. He should first spell the base word, *camp*, and then make it past tense by adding ed.

This next exercise will provide practice in identifying the base word.

"I will tell you the **past tense** word, and you will tell me the **base** word."

"The word is chopped." *Chop.*

Repeat this exercise using words on the back of the Key Card until your student can easily identify the base word. Note that your student is not spelling these words; he is only giving you the base word.

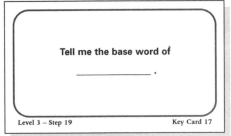

Tell me the base word of

_____ .

Level 3 – Step 19   Key Card 17

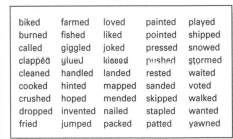

biked	farmed	loved	painted	played
burned	fished	liked	pointed	shipped
called	giggled	joked	pressed	snowed
clapped	glued	kissed	pushed	stormed
cleaned	handled	landed	rested	waited
cooked	hinted	mapped	sanded	voted
crushed	hoped	mended	skipped	walked
dropped	invented	nailed	stapled	wanted
fried	jumped	packed	patted	yawned

Place the Key Card behind the Review divider.

New Teaching
(continued)

Apply Key Card 14: Teach How to Add Suffix ED

"When you spell a past tense word, first spell the base word."

"I want to spell the word *jumped*. First I spell the base word, *jump*."

"Then I add suffix <u>ed</u>."

"Sometimes, when we add suffix <u>ed</u>, the 1-1-1 Rule applies. Let's review this Key Card."

Review Key Card 14 with your student.

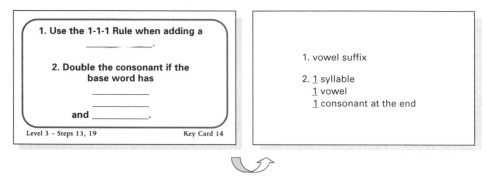

1. Use the 1-1-1 Rule when adding a

   _____.

2. Double the consonant if the base word has

   _____
   _____
   and _____.

Level 3 – Steps 13, 19   Key Card 14

1. vowel suffix

2. <u>1</u> syllable
   <u>1</u> vowel
   <u>1</u> consonant at the end

"I want to spell the word *shopped*. First I spell the base word, *shop*."

"Does the 1-1-1 Rule apply?" *Help your student see that it **does** apply. The word has 1 syllable, 1 vowel, and 1 consonant at the end.*

"So we need to double the <u>p</u> before adding the suffix."

Using the letter tiles and the <u>ed</u> suffix tile, have your student spell the following words. The student should first decide whether the 1-1-1 Rule applies, and then add the suffix.

wanted	**pointed**	**snowed**	**cleaned**
patted	**rested**	**mapped**	**waited**
clapped	**dropped**		

New Teaching
(continued)

Teach about Irregular Words

Build the word *run*. r u n

"With most words, we form the past tense by adding <u>ed</u>. But this doesn't work for **all** words."

"Finish this sentence. Today I **run**. Yesterday I _____." *Ran.*

Change the word *run* to *ran*. r a n

Give more examples, having your student complete the sentence.

"Today I **make**. Yesterday I _____." *Made.*

"Today I **swim**. Yesterday I _____." *Swam.*

"Today I **give**. Yesterday I _____." *Gave.*

Silent E Book: Identify the Job of Silent E

"Next I will show you a word that contains silent <u>e</u>. See if you can figure out where to put it in your Silent E Book."

Build the word *were*. w er e

Lead your student to see that *were* contains a Handyman E.

"Enter the word *were* in your Silent E Book on page 5."

Word Cards 121-130: Spell on Paper

Dictate the words and have your student spell them on paper.

121. pushed
122. shopped
123. wanted
124. pointed
125. snowed
126. waited   Amy waited for her sister.
127. dropped
128. cleaned
129. turned
130. were

> **Tip!**
>
> In the word *waited*, the <u>t</u> sounds like a <u>d</u> in the normal rhythm of speech. If your student spells the base word, *wait*, he will hear that it is spelled with a <u>t</u>.
>
> "Pronounce to spell" this word, enunciating the <u>t</u> for spelling purposes.

Place Word Cards 121-130 behind the Review divider.

Reinforcement

Dictate Sentences

Dictate several sentences each day.

The elk pushed a rock with his nose.

We shopped for dog food and catnip.

Dan wanted to go sledding.

Frank pointed his finger at me.

Last year it snowed for a week!

I waited for my turn at bat.

Sam dropped a toy truck on his feet.

The tiger cleaned his paws.

The lady turned to speak to Ted.

Were you helping Amy?

The brave man pointed to the sky.

We were camping for three days.

Writing Station

Dictate each word. Have your student say and write the base word, add the suffix, and write original sentences using the new words.

playing   sunny   swimming   mostly   lakes

Is the daily review helping your student internalize all the concepts he's learned so far? Are the decks behind the Mastered dividers getting bigger? Does your student have a firm grasp on the Key Card rules for spelling?

Mastered cards will be reviewed again in Step 22 to keep them fresh in your student's mind.

This lesson will teach that when you add a vowel suffix to a word ending in silent e, you drop the e before adding the suffix.

You will need: Key Card 18, Word Cards 131-140

Review

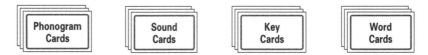

Word Bank for OA/OW

Word Analysis

p | i | ck | ed   "Read this word." *Picked.*

"How many syllables are in this word?" *One.*

"What is the last sound you hear?" */t/.*

"How is the /t/ sound spelled?" *Ed.*

"What is the base word?" *Pick.*

"What is the suffix?" *Ed.*

New Teaching

Teach Key Card 18: The Drop the E Rule

Sort suffixes into two piles: vowel suffixes and consonant suffixes.

Build the word *drive.*

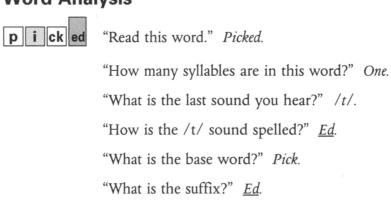

"When we add a **consonant suffix** to a word that ends in silent e, we don't need to make any changes. We just add the consonant suffix."

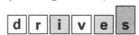

Remove the s, leaving the base word. "But if we add a **vowel suffix** to this, we need to follow the **Drop the E Rule**."

"I want to turn *drive* into *driving*. Ing is a vowel suffix, so first I have to drop the e…"

| d | r | i | v | | e |

"…and then add the suffix." | d | r | i | v | ing |

"Divide this word into syllables." *Student divides the word.*

| d | r | i | | v | ing |

"If I hadn't dropped the e…" Insert the e and push syllables together.

| d | r | i | v | e | ing |

"…there would be an extra vowel in this syllable. So we follow the **Drop the E Rule**."

Build the word *name*. | n | a | m | e |

"Change this word to *named*." *Student drops the e and adds ed.*

> If student doesn't drop the e first before adding ed, have him divide the word into syllables. Help him to see that there are too many vowels in the second syllable.   **Tip!**

Use the letter and vowel suffix tiles to practice this concept with the following words.

Build this word	Change to this word
trade	trader
give	giving
time	timer
fire	fired
note	noting

New Teaching
(continued)

Read Key Card 18 with your student, then file it behind the Review divider.

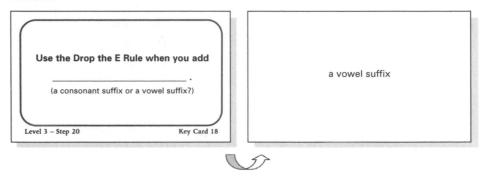

Provide Practice with Adding Vowel and Consonant Suffixes

Build the word *joke*.

"I want to change the word *joke* into *jokes*." j o k e s

"We have to leave the e there, because if we didn't…" Remove the e.

j o k s

"…what would this word say?" *Student replies /jŏks/.*

Replace the e.

"So you can see that the **Drop the E Rule** is needed **only** when we add **vowel suffixes**."

Have your student practice this concept, using the following words:

Build this word	Change to this word
joke	joking
joke	joker
tire	tires
brave	bravely
place	placed
smile	smiling
care	careful
dare	daring
love	lovely
use	used
use	useful
note	notes
ride	riding

Teach a Strategy for Spelling Words Containing Suffixes

"There are four steps you should follow every time you have to spell a word ending in a suffix. Let's practice them."

"First, listen to the word I dictate: *used.*"

"Second, say the base word." *Use.*

"Third, spell the base word." *Student spells the word with tiles.* [u][s][e]

"And fourth, add the suffix. Make sure you use the **Drop the E Rule** if you need to." *Student drops the e and adds suffix ed.*

[u][s][ed]

> Have your student use this strategy for spelling words with suffixes until he has completely mastered this concept.
> 1. <u>Hear</u> the dictated word.
> 2. <u>Say</u> the base word.
> 3. <u>Spell</u> the base word.
> 4. <u>Add</u> a suffix, applying a rule if necessary.
>
> You will need to prompt your student to follow the steps until they become routine.

Silent E Book: Identify the Job of Silent E

Build the word *come.* [c][o][m][e]

"The word *come* has a silent <u>e</u>. It probably used to be pronounced a long time ago."

Point to the <u>o</u>. "What sound does the <u>o</u> have in this word?" *Student replies /ŭ/.*

"In these next two words, the <u>o</u> also has the sound of /ŭ/."

Build the word *some.* [s][o][m][e]

"This word says…" *Some.*

Build the word *none.* [n][o][n][e]

"This word says…" *None.*

New Teaching
(continued)

Take out the Silent E Book. "Which page do these words belong on?"

Help the student to see that they belong on page 5, under Handyman E, since they do not belong under the other four categories. *Student records the words* come, some, *and* none.

Word Cards 131-140: Spell on Paper

Dictate the words and have your student spell them on paper.

131. **hoping**

132. **careful**

133. **using**

134. **wider**

135. **placed**

136. **smiled**

137. **glued**

138. **come**

139. **some**   Do you want some cake?

140. **none**   None of my socks have holes.

> **Tip!**
> If the student misses any of these words, have him follow the four-step strategy for adding suffixes, and apply the **Drop the E Rule** if necessary.

Place Word Cards 131-140 behind the Review divider.

Reinforcement

Dictate Sentences

Dictate several sentences each day.

Be careful when using a drill!

I was hoping to blow some bubbles.

Are you using that pencil?

The river is much wider here.

Jim placed a flag on his bike.

She smiled at the cheerful student.

I glued the paper to my hand!

Will you come to my party?

Do you want some toast?

None of the hotdogs have buns.

Bring your sled when you come over.

I gave none of the food to my goat.

Writing Station

Dictate each word. Have your student say and write the base word, add the suffix, and write original sentences using the new words.

taking **making** **crafts** **lately** **biggest**

Step 20: The Drop the E Rule

Step 21 – The /er/ of *First*

This lesson will teach the third most common spelling of the sound of /er/: ir.

You will need: Word Bank for IR, Word Cards 141-150

Review

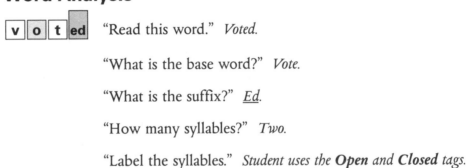

Word Bank for AI/AY
Word Bank for EA

Word Analysis

v o t ed   "Read this word." *Voted.*

"What is the base word?" *Vote.*

"What is the suffix?" *Ed.*

"How many syllables?" *Two.*

"Label the syllables." *Student uses the* **Open** *and* **Closed** *tags.*

New Teaching

Teach Another Way to Spell /er/

Build the words *winter* and *burn*.   w i n t er   b ur n

"You have learned several ways to spell the sound of /er/. Point to the letter tile that shows the /er/ of *her*." *Student points to the* er *tile in the word* winter.

"Good. Point to the letter tile that shows the /er/ of *nurse*." *Student points to the* ur *tile in the word* burn.

"You have also learned another phonogram that makes the sound of /er/. Pull down that tile." *Student pulls down the* ir *tile.*

New Teaching
(continued)

"Today we will work on spelling words with the sound of /er/ spelled ir."

Build the word *dirt*.   d | ir | t

"What does this word say?" *Dirt.*

"Good. I will dictate some words. The /er/ sound in these words is spelled with the ir tile."

Dictate the following words:

birth   **shirt**   **bird**   **third**

Introduce the Word Bank for IR

Have your student read through the **Word Bank for IR** to improve visual memory. We want students to become very familiar with the words in this Word Bank before the next spelling for /er/ is introduced.

Label Syllable Types

Build the following words with letter tiles. Have your student divide the words into syllables, if appropriate, and label with the proper syllable tag.

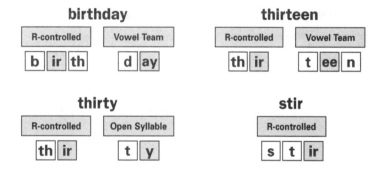

Reinforcement

Word Cards 141-150: Spell on Paper

Dictate the words and have your student spell them on paper.

141. girl
142. birthday
143. shirt
144. bird
145. dirt
146. circle
147. first
148. third
149. thirteen
150. thirty ("Pronounce for spelling." Enunciate the t for correct spelling.)

Place Word Cards 141-150 behind the Review divider.

More Words

birth   sir   firm   stir   skirt

Dictate Sentences

Dictate several sentences each day.

My third birthday was so fun!
I am drawing a circle in the dirt.
Sir Ben has a white shirt on.
The birth of the baby made me happy.
The dirt is firm under my feet.
When will you turn thirteen?
That girl has thirty pink dresses.
Did you stir the drink with a spoon?
A gentle bird sat on my arm.
This is her first day of school.
Is your birthday in April or May?
The bird will fly in a circle all day.

Reinforcement
(continued)

Adding Suffixes

1. Hear the dictated word.
2. Say the base word.
3. Spell the base word.
4. Add suffix, applying a rule if necessary.

Writing Station

Dictate each word. Have your student say and write the base word, add the suffix, and write original sentences using the new words.

stirring   **tables**   **baking**   **handful**   **setting**

Step 22 – Ways to Spell /er/

In this lesson, your student will analyze three ways to spell the sound of /er/.

You will need: Sound Card 58

Review

Word Bank for UR
Word Bank for IR

Quickly review the cards behind the Mastered dividers.

Word Analysis

"Divide this word into syllables." *Student counts back three tiles and divides.*

"The first syllable says…?" */cir/.*

"Is the first c hard or soft?" *Soft.*

"Why is the c soft?" *It is followed by an i.*

"The second syllable says…?" */cl/.*

"Is the second c hard or soft?" *Hard.*

"What is the reason for the silent e?" *To add a vowel to the last syllable.*

"Label the syllable types." *Student uses the R-controlled and C+le tags.*

New Teaching
(continued)

Introduce the Word Sort for /er/ Chart

Write these three headings across the top of lined paper. Draw vertical lines to form three columns:

<u>er</u>	<u>ur</u>	<u>ir</u>

Point to the column headings. "Here are three ways to spell the sound of /er/."

Give your student a new sheet of lined paper. "I will dictate a word, and you will write it down on your paper. When you are satisfied that you have spelled the word correctly, copy the word to the correct column on this chart."

Dictate these words:

nurse	**first**	**sister**	**return**	**thirteen**
purple	**church**	**farmer**	**printer**	**older**

Teach Sound Card 58

"Today we have a new Sound Card."

Read Sound Card 58:

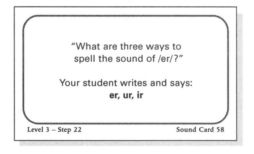

"What are three ways to
spell the sound of /er/?"

Your student writes and says:
er, ur, ir

Level 3 – Step 22   Sound Card 58

"Write and say the three ways like this." Say the names of the letters as you write them down: "<u>er</u>, <u>ur</u>, and <u>ir</u>."

Practice this Sound Card with your student, and then store it behind the Review divider.

Reinforcement

Dictate Sentences

Dictate several sentences each day.

His fur is full of dirt.

Will my birthday ever come?

Did you burn your finger?

Bob can throw a super curve ball!

I have a large number of birds.

The river is frozen in the winter.

My sister hurt herself.

Sue will come over after church.

That girl can turn the printer on.

Please return to the circle.

Never disturb Sir Ben!

Her team has thirteen members.

Writing Station

Dictate each word. Have your student say and write the base word, add the suffix, and write original sentences using the new words.

farmer **milking** **living** **wagged** **littlest**

Step 23 – The Sound of /ŏŏ/ Spelled OO

In this lesson, your student will learn words that contain the sound of /ŏŏ/ spelled oo.

You will need: yellow pencil, jail, Homophones List, Word Cards 151-160

Review

| Phonogram Cards | Sound Cards | Key Cards | Word Cards |

Word Bank for IR

Word Analysis

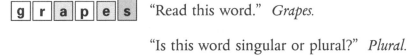

| g | r | a | p | e | s |

"Read this word." *Grapes.*

"Is this word singular or plural?" *Plural.*

"What sound does the letter <u>a</u> represent?" */ā/.*

"What sound does the letter <u>e</u> represent?" *None. It is silent.*

"Why can't we leave out the silent <u>e</u>?" *Then the word would say "graps."*

"How many syllables?" *One.*

"Label the syllable". *Student uses the VCE tag.*

New Teaching

Teach the Sound of /ŏŏ/ Spelled OO

Pull down the <u>oo</u> tile. | oo |

"Tell me the three sounds of this tile." */ōō/ - /ŏŏ/ - /ō/.*

Build the word *good.* | g | oo | d |

"In this word, <u>oo</u> says its second sound, /ŏŏ/. What is this word?" *Good.*

"Yes. Listen for the /ŏŏ/ sound: *good…/ŏŏ/.*"

"Today you will learn words with the /ŏŏ/ sound. I will dictate some words. When you hear the sound of /ŏŏ/, spell it with the <u>oo</u> tile."

Dictate the following words:

wood   **shook**   **stood**   **look**

Teach a Rule Breaker

"If there are twin babies, how many babies are there?" *Two.*

Build the word *twin.*

"What are the first two letters of the word *twin?*" *T-<u>w</u>.*

"If the phone rings twice, how many times does it ring?" *Two times.*

Change the word to *twice.*

"What are the first two letters of the word *twice?*" *T-<u>w</u>.*

"One plus one is…?" *Two.*

Change the word to *two.*

"What are the first two letters of the word *two?*" *T-<u>w</u>.*

"We spell the word *two* with <u>t-w</u>, but we don't hear the <u>w</u>. *Two* is a Rule Breaker."

Take out Word Card 160. Have your student circle the <u>w</u>, fill it in with yellow pencil, and put the card in jail.

"Spell the word *two,* as in *two puppies.*" *Student spells the word.*

Step 23: The Sound of /ŏŏ/ Spelled OO

New Teaching
(continued)

Homophones List: Add the Word *Two*

"*Two,* as in *two puppies,* is a homophone. Add it to your Homophones List next to *to* and *too.*" *Student writes the word.*

Read the following sentences and have your student point to the correct word on the Homophones List.

> **The car has <u>two</u> flat tires.**
> **Would you like <u>to</u> go <u>to</u> the movies with me?**
> **Matt can go, <u>too</u>.**
> **I made <u>two</u> sandwiches for our picnic.**
> **Let's swim <u>to</u> the island.**
> **It is <u>too</u> hot for running.**

Teach the Words *There* and *Very*

"Spell the word *here* with tiles. *Here,* as in *come here.*" *Student spells the word.*

| h | e | r | e |

"We can change the word *here* to *there*. *There*, as in *over there*." Replace the <u>h</u> tile with the <u>th</u> tile.

| th | e | r | e |

Tip!

If the word *there* gives your student any trouble, you can put it in jail. The <u>e</u> is usually considered a short <u>e</u>, but in the normal rhythm of speech, the <u>r</u> distorts the vowel sound. In many regions the vowel sound "slides" from /ĕ/ to /ā/.

You can either tell your student to "pronounce for spelling" or treat the word like a Rule Breaker.

Build the word *very*.

| v | e | r | y |

"*Very* is another word on your spelling list today."

The vowel sound in the word *very* is similar to that in the word *there*. Again, if it gives your student trouble at any time, you can tell your student to "pronounce for spelling" or treat the word like a Rule Breaker.

Silent E Book: Identify the Job of Silent E

Take out the Silent E Book. Have your student determine the page on which to enter these words:

here (pg. 1)   **there** (pg. 5)

Word Cards 151-160: Spell on Paper

Dictate the words and have your student spell them on paper.

151. look
152. cook
153. book
154. good
155. wood   My uncle chops wood.
156. foot
157. took
158. very
159. there   Your book is over there.
160. two   Two fish swam in the tank.

Place Word Cards 151-160 behind the Review divider.

Reinforcement

More Words

stood   shook   hook   childhood

Reinforcement
(continued)

Dictate Sentences
Dictate several sentences each day.

Look at all the stars in the sky!

Mom is a very good cook.

Did you read that new book?

I got good grades this year.

Kim made a fishing pole of wood.

Is there a fish on the hook?

Ed took his sister to the park.

This is a very useful book.

I see two boats over there.

She stood on her left foot.

My childhood has been cheerful.

I shook the snow from the tree.

Writing Station

Dictate each word. Have your student say and write the base word, add the suffix, and write original sentences using the new words.

cleaning   **dirty**   **bubbles**   **soapy**   **mopped**

Step 24 – Three-Letter I

This lesson will teach words with the sound of /ī/ spelled igh.

You will need: Word Cards 161-170

Review

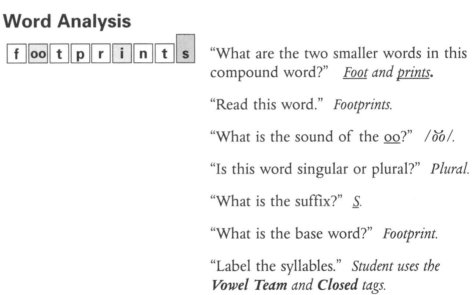

Word Bank for OA/OW
Word Bank for EA

Word Analysis

| f | oo | t | p | r | i | n | t | s |

"What are the two smaller words in this compound word?" *Foot* and *prints*.

"Read this word." *Footprints*.

"What is the sound of the oo?" /ŏŏ/.

"Is this word singular or plural?" *Plural*.

"What is the suffix?" *S*.

"What is the base word?" *Footprint*.

"Label the syllables." *Student uses the* **Vowel Team** *and* **Closed** *tags.*

New Teaching

Teach Another Way to Spell /ī/

Build the words *tiger, bite,* and *cry*.

| t | i | g | er | | b | i | t | e | | c | r | y |

"You have learned several ways to spell the sound of /ī/."

Divide the word *tiger* into syllables. | t | i | | g | er |

New Teaching
(continued)

"Why is the i̲ long in the word *tiger*?" *Because it is at the end of a syllable.*

"Good. The first way to spell the sound of /ī/ is to put it in an open syllable."

Point to the word *bite*. "Why is the i̲ long in the word *bite*?" *Because of the silent e̲.*

"Right. The second way to spell the sound of /ī/ is to add a silent e̲."

Point to the word *cry*. "Why is the i̲ long in the word *cry*?" *English words don't end in i̲, so we use a y̲.*

"Right. The third way to spell the sound of /ī/ is to use a y̲."

"You have also learned another phonogram that makes the sound of /ī/. Pull down that tile." *Student pulls down the ig̲h̲ tile.*

"Today we will work on spelling words with the sound of /ī/ spelled ig̲h̲."

Build the word light. ｜ l ｜ igh ｜ t ｜

"What does this word say?" *Light.*

"Change *light* to *right*." ｜ r ｜ igh ｜ t ｜

Build the word *tonight*. ｜ t ｜ o ｜ n ｜ igh ｜ t ｜

"To spell the word *tonight*, we need to **pronounce for spelling**. When we speak, we normally say *tonight*."

Point to the o̲. "But when we pronounce the word for spelling, we need to pronounce the /ōō/ sound clearly: *Too-night*."

"I will dictate some words. The /ī/ sound in these words is spelled with the ig̲h̲ tile."

Have your student spell these words with tiles:

night   **high**   **sight**   **might**   **fight**

Teach the Words *They* and *House*

Build the word *they*.

Point to the ey. "In the word *they*, what sound does the ey tile make?" /ā/.

Build the word *house*.

Point to the ou tile. "In the word *house*, what sound does this tile make?" /ow/.

"The e is silent in the word *house*. Identify the reason and write this word in your Silent E Book." *Student writes the word on page 5.*

Word Cards 161-170: Spell on Paper

Dictate the words and have your student spell them on paper.

161. night It rained all night.
162. right Use your right hand.
163. high The mountain is very high.
164. might I might go with you.
165. light
166. tonight
167. sight A sunset is a beautiful sight.
168. fight
169. they
170. house

Place Word Cards 161-170 behind the Review divider.

Reinforcement

Dictate Sentences

Dictate several sentences each day.

It was cold and windy last night.

Are you standing on your right foot?

The cake is too high to reach!

You might like my garden.

There is a moth near the light.

The spy will meet you tonight.

The old dog lost his sight.

That fox had a fight with the hen!

Please put this in the house.

They will fly south this winter.

Tonight there is a thick fog.

Do you think they were right?

Writing Station

Dictate each word. Have your student say and write the base word, add the suffix, and write original sentences using the new words.

lighting   candles   windows   flames   foggy

Step 25 – Ways to Spell /ī/

In this lesson, your student will analyze four ways to spell the sound of /ī/.

You will need: Sound Card 59

Review

Phonogram Cards   Sound Cards   Key Cards   Word Cards

Word Bank for IR

Word Analysis

| u | n | d | er | s | t | oo | d |

"Read this word." *Understood.*

"How many syllables?" *Three.*

"What are the two smaller words in this compound word?" *Under and stood.*

"Divide between the two words." *Student divides.*

"Divide the word *under*." *Student divides between the n and d.*

"What represents the /er/ sound?" *Er.*

"Label the syllable types." *Student uses the Closed, R-controlled, and Vowel Team tags.*

New Teaching

Introduce the Word Sort for /ī/ Chart

Write these four headings across the top of lined paper. Draw vertical lines to form four columns:

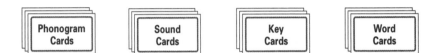

i	i-e	y	igh

Point to the column headings. "Here are four ways to spell the sound of /ī/."

Give your student a new sheet of lined paper. "I will dictate a word, and you will write it down on your paper. When you are satisfied that you have spelled the word correctly, copy the word to the correct column on this chart."

Dictate these words:

tiny	**dime**	**light**	**cry**	**tiger**
behind	**sly**	**nineteen**	**tonight**	**while**

Teach Sound Card 59

"Today we have a new Sound Card."

Read Sound Card 59:

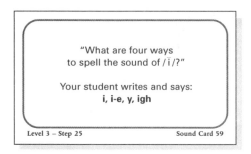

"What are four ways
to spell the sound of /ī/?"

Your student writes and says:
i, i-e, y, igh

Level 3 – Step 25   Sound Card 59

"Write and say the four ways like this." Say the letters as you write them down: "i, i-consonant-e, y, and igh." Remind your student that we write a *dash* for the word *consonant*.

Practice this Sound Card with your student, and then store it behind the Review divider.

More spellings of long i include:

• y-e as in *rhyme*
• ie as in *tie*
• ei as in *height*

These spellings aren't used in nearly as many words as the four we studied today and will be covered at a later time.

Step 25: Ways to Spell /ī/

Reinforcement

Dictate Sentences

Dictate several sentences each day.

Try to drive on the right side!

At night I hear the wild cry of a tiny cat.

Light the fire while I fry the fish.

These fine gold items are mine.

The hawk is high in the silent sky.

The child will hide under the slide.

Did you ride for nine miles?

Why did Ken fight this time?

I might find a pile of wire.

His wife is kind and quite shy.

The bee will fly to the hive tonight.

Did those blind bats bite my bird?

Writing Station

Dictate each word. Have your student say and write the base word, add the suffix, and write original sentences using the new words.

driver   safely   passes   filling   waved

Step 26 – The Change the Y to I Rule

In this lesson, your student will learn the rules for adding suffixes to words ending in y.

You will need: Key Card 19, Word Cards 171-180

Review

Word Analysis

   "Read this word." *Spray.*

"How is the sound of /ā/ spelled?" *Ay.*

"Is the y alone or part of a vowel team?" *Part of a vowel team.*

"Label this syllable." *Student uses the **Vowel Team** tag.*

New Teaching

Explain the Term *Single Vowel Y*

Place the following tiles in front of the student:

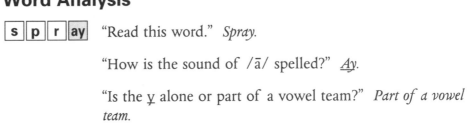

Point to the y. "This is a *single vowel y*. **Single** means **one**. There is just **one** letter on this tile, so we say that it is a **single vowel y**."

Point to the other tiles. "These tiles have a y, but not a **single vowel y**."

New Teaching
(continued)

Teach Key Card 19: The Change the Y to I Rule

Build the word *cry*. | c | r | y |

"I want to change *cry* to *cried*. Which suffix would I use?" *Suffix ed.*

"Right. Pull down ed. What letter does the word *cry* end in?" *The letter y.*

"Is it a single vowel y?" *Yes.*

"We have a rule in English that says that if a word ends in single vowel y, we have to do something special before we add the suffix."

Exchange the y tile for an i. "We have to change the y to an i..."

"...and then add the suffix." | c | r | i | ed |

"Now you try it. The word is *dried*. What is the base word?" *Dry.*

"Spell the base word." *Student spells the word with tiles.* | d | r | y |

"Does the word end in a **single vowel y**?" *Yes.*

"So what do you need to do?" *Student changes the y to an i, and adds the suffix.*

"Good. We call this rule the **Change the Y to I Rule**."

Build the word *stay*. | s | t | ay |

"When there are two letters on a tile, they don't like to be broken up. They are a team. Teams like to stay together."

"I want to change the word *stay* to *stayed*. I just add the suffix ed."

| s | t | ay | ed |

"I don't change the y to i, because this team wants to stay together."

"We only use the **Change the Y to I Rule** with a **single vowel y**."

New Teaching
(continued)

Provide Mixed Practice

Have your student practice this concept by building these words with the letter and suffix tiles.

Build this word	Is there a Single Y?	Change to this word
fry	Yes	fried
try	Yes	tried
play	No	player
pay	No	payment
windy	Yes	windier
joy	No	joyful
dry	Yes	driest
tray	No	trays
copy	Yes	copier

> If you sense that your student needs more time to let this concept "sink in," this is a good stopping spot. You may wish to stop here for today, and continue with the rest of the lesson tomorrow.
>
> If your student understands the concepts taught so far, continue on. The second half of the **Change the Y to I Rule** will be taught next.

Teach about Adding Suffixes Beginning with I

Build the word *try*. [t][r][y]

"We change **single vowel y** to an i before adding a suffix, except in one case."

Build the word *trying*. [t][r][y][ing]

Point to suffix ing. "If the suffix you are adding starts with i, **don't** change the y to i."

"If I change the y to i by mistake, the word will look like this."

"In English, we don't put two i's together."

We **do** have two i's together in the word *skiing*, but *ski* is a Scandinavian word. Sometimes foreign words are assimilated into our language so quickly that they are not changed to conform to English rules.

Have your student practice this concept with the following words.

Build this word	Change to this word
cry	**crying**
fly	**flying**
dry	**drying**

"Why didn't you change the y to i?" *Because there would have been two i's in a row. (Or, we don't change the y to i when we add ing.)*

Take out Key Card 19 and read it with your student:

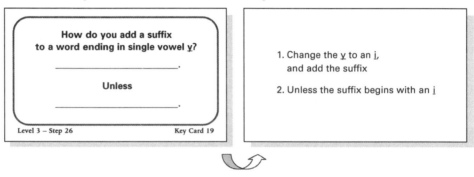

Teach about Adding Suffix ES

Build the word *cry*. [c][r][y]

"I want to spell the word *cries*. The last letter is a **single vowel y**, so I change the y to i."

"If I add an s to make the word *cries*..."

[c][r][i][s]

"...something is wrong. This becomes a closed syllable. In a closed syllable, would this vowel be long or short?" *Short.*

"Right. What would this word say?" /crĭs/.

"So we can't just add s to make the word *cries*. We need to add suffix es."

[c][r][i][es]

Step 26: The Change the Y to I Rule

New Teaching
(continued)

Have your student practice this concept with the following words.

Build this word	Change to this word
dry	dries
try	tries
baby	babies

"Why didn't you just add an s after you changed the y to i?" *Because it would have made the vowel short, and we want to keep the vowel long.*

Word Cards 171-180: Spell with Tiles

To give your student more practice with the **Change the Y to I Rule**, first have him spell the words using the letter and suffix tiles.

171. pennies

172. crying

173. fries

174. playful

175. happier

176. babies

177. payment

178. windiest

179. candies

180. tried

> **Tip!** If your student is having trouble with these concepts, have him build the base word first, then apply the rules on Key Card 19 to add the suffix.

Spell on Paper

Once your student is able to spell the words using the tiles, dictate Word Cards 171-180 and have him spell the words on paper.

Place Word Cards 171-180 behind the Review divider.

Reinforcement

More Words

copier	dries	driest	drying	flying
fried	joyful	player	trays	tries

Reinforcement
(continued)

Dictate Sentences
Dictate several sentences each day.

My dog tried to eat my pennies!

Why is Ted crying?

Dad fries the clams.

Are the sheep very playful?

I feel happier when I read.

Babies make me feel joyful.

Ed made a big payment today.

This is the windiest hilltop.

How many candies are on those trays?

She tries to spray me with water!

August is the driest time of year.

Are you the best player on the team?

Adding Suffixes

1. <u>Hear</u> the dictated word.
2. <u>Say</u> the base word.
3. <u>Spell</u> the base word.
4. <u>Add suffix</u>, applying a <u>rule</u> if necessary.

Writing Station

Dictate each word. Have your student say and write the base word, add the suffix, and write original sentences using the new words.

snowy   **sliding**   **trying**   **sledding**   **hopeful**

Step 27 – Contractions

In this lesson, your student will learn common contractions.

You will need: rubber band, apostrophe tile, Word Cards 181-190

Review

Word Analysis

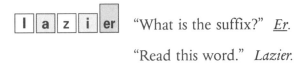

"What is the suffix?" *Er.*

"Read this word." *Lazier.*

"What is the base word?" *Lazy.*

"The word *lazy* ends in a *y*. What happened to the *y*?" *Before adding a suffix, you change the *y* to an *i*.*

"How many syllables are in this word?" *Three.*

"Divide into syllables." *Student divides before the *z* and before the *er*.*

"Label the syllables." *Student uses the **Open**, **Open**, and **R-controlled** tags.*

New Teaching

Introduce Contractions

In this exercise, you will use a rubber band to demonstrate the meaning of the words *contract* and *expand*. When you say the word *expand*, stretch the rubber band out.

"A rubber band can **expand** and **contract**. Watch: **Expand**. **Contract**." Demonstrate the concept with the rubber band.

"When is the rubber band smaller, when it **expands** or when it **contracts**?" *When it contracts.*

New Teaching
(continued)

"Today you are going to learn some contractions. A contraction is **two** words that are made into **one** word. Say the word *contraction*." *Contraction.*

"We call it a *contraction* because the words **contract** and become smaller."

"Here is an example." Build the words *he* and *is*.

| h | e | | i | s |

Remove the i and replace it with the apostrophe. "Instead of two words, **he is**, we now have one word, **he's**."

| h | e | ' | s |

"This is called a **contraction**."

Point to the apostrophe tile. "I put an **apostrophe** in place of the letter that I took out. Say the word *apostrophe*." *Apostrophe.*

Build the words *she* and *will*. | sh | e | | w | i | l | l |

"I can say, *She will come over,* or I can use a shortcut and say, *She'll come over.*"

Change *she will* into *she'll*. | sh | e | ' | l | l |

"**She'll** is a contraction, a shorter way of saying **she will**."

Remove the apostrophe. | sh | e | l | l |

"What happens if I forget to put in the apostrophe? What word do we have?" *Shell.*

"That's not the word we want. So you can see that it is important to put in the apostrophe." Replace the apostrophe.

Teach Common Contractions

Using the letter tiles, build the two words in the first column, and then show your student how to create the contraction using the apostrophe tile. Do the first few together, then let your student try it alone. Reading the sentences with your student will help illustrate how contractions look and sound in a sentence.

Two words	Contraction	Sentence
she is	she's	She's my sister.
he is	he's	He's fifteen years old.
that is	that's	That's an extra slice of pizza.
is not	isn't	Isn't this a friendly dog?
do not	don't	Don't knock the glass over!
cannot	can't	Jenny can't drive yet.
did not	didn't	It didn't rain last night.
I will	I'll	I'll go with you to the park.
he will	he'll	He'll like this present.
she will	she'll	She'll need a winter coat.
we will	we'll	We'll keep you company.
you will	you'll	You'll enjoy the book.
I am	I'm	I'm very thirsty.

Store the apostrophe tile under the following label:

Other Tiles

'

New Teaching
(continued)

Word Cards 181-190: Spell on Paper

Dictate the words and have your student spell them on paper.

181. I'll   I'll call you later.

182. can't

183. didn't

184. he's

185. don't

186. that's

187. isn't

188. she'll

189. you'll   You'll be done soon.

190. she's

Place Word Cards 181-190 behind the Review divider.

Reinforcement

More Words

I'm   **we'll**   **he'll**

Dictate Sentences

Dictate several sentences each day.

I'll see you at my house.

Pam can't come over today.

We'll go sledding soon.

She didn't clean her room.

I don't have any more candy.

You'll find the toy over there.

Isn't that a priceless doll?

That's a very good book!

She's a fun girl!

I'm doing a math problem.

He's got a song she'll like.

He'll sing all day and night!

Reinforcement
(continued)

Writing Station

Dictate each word. Have your student say and write the base word, add the suffix, and write original sentences using the new words.

eventful   **tipping**   **stormy**   **windier**   **crashes**

Step 28 – Homophones

In this lesson, your student will learn how to spell common pairs of homophones.

You will need: Homophones List, More Sets of Homophones sheet, Word Cards 191-200

Review

Review All Word Banks

Review the cards behind the Mastered dividers. This is the last review for Level Three, so make it thorough!

Word Analysis

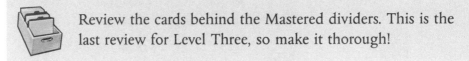

"Read this word." *We'll.*

"What two words were used to form this contraction?" *We will.*

"What letters were left out to form this contraction?" <u>*W-i.*</u>

"What would happen if we forgot the apostrophe?" *It would say* well.

New Teaching

Introduce Homophone Pairs

Take out the Homophones List.

"You have written homophones on your list. What are homophones?" *Words that sound alike but are spelled differently.*

"Right. Let's look again at the homophones you've written. I'll dictate a sentence, and you'll point to the correct word on your list."

Use the following sentences, making sure your student points to the correct word.

She has <u>four</u> marbles.
I'm going <u>to</u> school.
Can you <u>hear</u> me?
I got this <u>for</u> you.
The music is <u>too</u> loud.
Will you come <u>here</u>?
He wrote <u>two</u> songs.

"Good. Today we will look at more homophone pairs."

Take out the More Sets of Homophones sheet.

Point to the words *be* and *bee*. "Point to the word I would use in this sentence: *The <u>bee</u> pollinated the flower.*" *Student points to* bee.

Continue like this for each pair of homophones to make sure your student can distinguish between the words. Use the following sentences:

be	What do you want to <u>be</u> when you grow up?
bee	The <u>bee</u> pollinated the flower.
dear	My friends are very <u>dear</u> to me.
deer	Did you see the <u>deer</u> on the hill?
ad	I saw an <u>ad</u> for candy yesterday.
add	Please <u>add</u> sugar to the cookie mix.
sea	It's fun to swim in the <u>sea</u>.
see	You can <u>see</u> the waves from here.
some	Would you like <u>some</u> fried clams?
sum	The <u>sum</u> of all the numbers is twenty.
aunt	My <u>aunt</u> is coming to dinner tonight.
ant	There is an <u>ant</u> on the kitchen table.
won	Her team <u>won</u> all three games.
one	My team only has <u>one</u> good player on it.
weak	Do you feel <u>weak</u> after you run?
week	It took a <u>week</u> to finish my homework.
male	Everyone in that group is <u>male</u>.
mail	Did you get the <u>mail</u> today?

Step 28: Homophones

New Teaching
(continued)

read	He <u>read</u> me a story from the newspaper.
red	I put a <u>red</u> flag on my bike.
sun	Don't look directly at the <u>sun</u>.
son	Her <u>son</u> is two years older than I am.

Homophones List: Add New Word Pairs

Have your student add the new homophone pairs to his Homophones List.

Word Cards 191-200: Spell on Paper

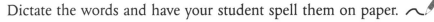

Dictate the words and have your student spell them on paper.

191. dear   He is a dear boy.
192. add   Add this word to your list.
193. sea   The sea is salty.
194. sum   What is the sum of all the numbers?
195. ant   The ant crawled up my leg.
196. male   Is that a male dog?
197. son   His son was stung by a bee.
198. won   We won the game.
199. weak   My arms are very weak.
200. read   I read the book yesterday.

Place Word Cards 191-200 behind the Review divider.

Reinforcement

More Words

ad   (advertisement)

Reinforcement
(continued)

Dictate Sentences

Dictate several sentences each day.

> **Too many candies will make you sick!**
> **She'll add some of the numbers.**
> **I love to find shells at the sea.**
> **What is the sum of three minus one?**
> **Did she see that red ant?**
> **Her son has a male child.**
> **The tiny bee sat on a plum.**
> **Sue won a prize in the mail.**
> **I am too weak to play in the sun!**
> **Come meet my dear aunt Beth.**
> **I read an ad in the paper last night.**
> **He won't be at the sea this year.**
> **I saw two deer last week.**

Writing Station

Dictate each word. Have your student say and write the base word, add the suffix, and write original sentences using the new words.

tiniest   holding   smiling   sweetly   looking

Celebrate!

Present Your Student with the Certificate of Achievement

Certificate of Achievement

awarded to

_____

for successfully completing

Spelling - Level Three

Teacher Signature_____   Date_____

Step 28: Homophones

3
Appendices

Phonograms Taught in Level Three

Phonograms are letters or letter combinations representing a single sound. For example, the letter <u>b</u> represents the sound /b/, as in *bat*. The letter combination <u>sh</u> represents the sound /sh/, as in *ship*.

Card #	Phonogram	Sound	For the Teacher's Use Only (example of word containing the phonogram)			Step
44	ay	/ā/, two-letter /ā/ that we **may** use at the end of English words	day			
45	ai	/ā/, two-letter /ā/ that we **may not** use at the end of English words	rain			Step 1
46	ur	/er/ as in *nurse*	nurse			
47	oa	/ō/, two-letter /ō/ that we **may not** use at the end of English words	boat			Step 6
48	oo	/o͞o/–/o͝o/–/ō/	school	book	door	
49	ea	/ē/–/ĕ/–/ā/	leaf	bread	great	Step 11
50	ed	/ed/–/d/–/t/	landed	pulled	baked	
51	igh	/ī/, three-letter /ī/	light			
52	ir	/er/ as in *first*	first			Step 18
53	ey	/ā/–/ē/ that we **may** use at the end of English words	they	key		

Scope and Sequence of Level Three

Your Student Will:	Step
Review concepts taught in previous levels	1
Learn phonograms <u>ai</u>, <u>ay</u>, and <u>ur</u>	1
Spell words with the sound of /ā/ spelled <u>ai</u> and <u>ay</u>	2
Analyze four ways to spell the sound of /ā/	3
Categorize the jobs of silent <u>e</u>	4
Identify a C+le syllable type	5
Identify the fourth job of silent <u>e</u>: to add a vowel to C+le syllables	5
Spell words with C+le syllables	5
Learn phonogram <u>oa</u>	6
Learn how to double consonants in C+le words	6
Learn about homophones	6
Spell words with double consonants	6
Learn the second most common spelling of the /er/ sound	7
Spell words with the sound of /er/ spelled <u>ur</u>	7
Identify the fifth job of silent <u>e</u>: Handyman E	7
Learn when <u>y</u> can say /ē/	8
Spell words with the ending sound of /ē/ spelled <u>y</u>	8
Learn when to use <u>oa</u> and when to use <u>ow</u> for /ō/	9
Spell words with the sound of /ō/ spelled <u>oa</u> and <u>ow</u>	9
Analyze four ways to spell the sound of /ō/	10
Learn phonograms <u>oo</u>, <u>ea</u>, <u>ed</u>	11
Learn how to add consonant suffixes	11
Spell words with consonant suffixes	11
Learn how to add vowel suffixes	12
Learn how to double consonants before a vowel suffix	12
Spell words with vowel suffixes	12
Learn the 1-1-1 Rule for adding suffixes	13
Spell words with consonant and vowel suffixes	13
Learn the six question words: *who, what, why, where, when, how*	14
Spell words beginning with <u>wh</u>	14
Spell words with the sound of /ōō/ spelled <u>oo</u>	15
Analyze four ways to spell the sound of /k/	16
Learn when to use <u>ea</u> for /ē/	17
Spell words with the sound of /ē/ spelled <u>ea</u>	17
Learn phonograms <u>igh</u>, <u>ir</u>, and <u>ey</u>	18
Analyze five ways to spell the sound of /ē/	18
Learn about past tense	19
Recognize the three sounds of suffix <u>ed</u>	19
Identify the base words of past tense words	19
Learn how to add the suffix <u>ed</u>	19
Learn the Drop the E Rule for adding vowel suffixes	20
Learn the third most common spelling of the /er/ sound	21
Spell words with the sound of /er/ spelled <u>ir</u>	21
Analyze three ways to spell the sound of /er/	22
Spell words with the sound of /ōō/ spelled <u>oo</u>	23
Spell words with the sound of /ī/ spelled <u>igh</u>	24
Analyze four ways to spell the sound of /ī/	25
Learn the concept of single vowel <u>y</u>	26
Learn the Change the Y to I Rule for adding suffixes	26
Learn how to add suffixes <u>ing</u> and <u>es</u> to words ending in <u>y</u>	26
Spell words using the Change the Y to I Rule	26
Spell common contractions	27
Spell common pairs of homophones	28

Words Taught in Level Three

The number listed corresponds with the Step in which the word is first introduced.

A
able 5
ad 28
add 28
Amy 8
ant 28
any 15
apple 6
are 7
army 8

B
babies 26
baby 8
baking 21
bedding 13
bee 28
biggest 20
bird 21
birth 21
birthday 21
blindness 11
blow 9
boat 9
body 8
boldly 11
bony 8
book 23
boxes 13
brushes 17
bubble 6
bubbles 23
burn 7

C
candies 26
candle 5
candles 24
candy 8
camping 12
can't 27
careful 20
cheerful 11
childhood 23
childish 12
chopping 12
church 7
circle 21
city 8
clay 2
clean 17
cleaned 19
cleaning 23
clear 17
coat 9
coats 11

coldest 12
coldness 11
come 20
cook 23
copier 26
copy 8
crafts 20
crashes 27
crispy 12
crow 9
crying 26
cupful 11
curl 7
curve 7
cuteness 11
cutting 12

D
darkness 11
darker 12
day 2
days 11
deal 17
dear 28
didn't 27
digging 13
dirt 21
dirty 23
disturb 7
doing 13
don't 27
drawing 13
dries 26
driest 26
dripping 14
driver 25
dropped 19
drying 26

E
each 17
ear 17
eat 17
eating 17
ending 12
eventful 27

F
fail 2
fair 2
farmer 22
fastest 12
feeding 15
fifty 8
fight 24
filling 25

firm 21
first 21
fishing 13
fitness 11
flames 24
float 9
flying 26
foam 9
foggy 24
food 15
foot 23
forgetful 11
forgiveness 11
forty 8
four 6
fried 26
fries 26
from 17
fur 7

G
gentle 5
getting 16
giggle 6
girl 21
gladly 11
gladness 11
glow 9
glued 20
goat 9
good 23
graceful 11
grassy 8
grow 9

H
handful 21
handle 5
handy 12
happier 26
happy 8
hardness 11
harmful 11
hear 17
he'll 27
helper 12
helping 12
helpful 11
he's 27
high 24
hilly 8
holding 28
hook 23
hopeful 26
hoping 20
house 24

hurt 7
hurtful 11

I
I'll 27
illness 11
I'm 27
inches 12
isn't 27

J
jail 2
jogger 12
joyful 26
jumping 13

K
keeping 13
kindness 11

L
lady 8
lately 20
lazy 8
lead 17
light 24
lighting 24
little 6
littlest 22
living 22
load 9
loan 9
look 23
looking 28
loudest 12
loudness 11
low 9
lucky 8

M
mail 2
mailbox 2
making 20
male 28
many 15
maple 5
marble 6
May 2
mean 17
melting 14
middle 6
might 24
milking 22
mindful 11
moistness 11
mopped 23

mopping 12
mostly 19
mouthful 11
muddy 13

N
napping 12
near 17
needle 6
night 24
none 20
noon 15
noses 17

O
oak 9
oily 12
oldest 12
once 11
one 11
only 11
own 8
owner 13

P
paint 2
papers 18
parking 13
party 8
passes 25
pavement 11
pay 2
payment 26
pennies 26
penny 8
petting 17
placed 20
placement 11
planning 12
play 2
player 26
playful 26
playing 19
plays 15
please 17
pointed 19
ponds 14
pony 8
pray 2
priceless 11
printing 12
puddle 6
puppy 8
purple 7
pushed 19
puzzle 6

Q
quickly 14

R
rain 2
rainy 14
ray 2
reach 17
read (present) 17
read (past tense) 28
reading 18
return 7
riches 12
right 24
ripeness 11
road 9
roads 11
room 15
rotting 12
runner 13
running 12

S
sadness 11
safely 25
said 5
sail 2
sailing 13
sandy 12
say 2
school 15
scrapes 11
sea 28
setting 21
sharpness 11
she'll 27
she's 27
shipment 11
shirt 21
shook 23
shopped 19
shopping 13
show 9
sight 24
silently 11
sipping 13
sir 21
sixty 8
skipping 13
skirt 21
sledding 26
sliding 26
slow 9
slower 13
smaller 16
smarter 18
smiled 20
smiling 28
snacking 16
snail 2
sniffs 17
snow 9
snowed 19
snowing 13

snowy 26
soak 9
soap 9
soapy 23
sobbing 15
some 20
son 28
soon 15
speak 17
spoon 15
spoonful 15
spotless 11
spray 2
standing 12
stands 11
staple 5
staples 18
stay 2
sticky 16
stiffness 11
stir 21
stirring 21
stood 23
stopping 12
stormy 27
strongest 12
sum 28
sunny 19
sweetly 28
sweetness 16
swimmer 12
swimming 19

T
table 5
tables 21
tail 2
taking 20
teach 17
teacher 18
team 17
thankful 11
that's 27
thawing 13
there 23
they 24
thickest 12
thickness 11
third 21
thirteen 21
thirty 21
throw 9
tiniest 28
tiny 8
tipping 27
title 5
toad 9
toast 9
today 2
tonight 24
too 15

took 23
tooth 15
toothless 15
trail 2
train 2
tray 2
trays 26
tried 26
tries 26
trying 26
turn 7
turned 19
two 23

U
ugly 8
uncle 5
useful 11
using 20

V
very 23

W
wagged 22
wait 2
waited 19
waiting 13
wanted 19
waved 25
way 2
weak 28
we'll 27
were 19
wetter 12
whale 14
what 14
wheel 14
when 14
where 14
which 14
whisper 14
white 14
who 14
whose 14
wider 20
windier 27
windiest 26
window 9
windows 24
windy 8
winner 13
winning 13
won 28
wood 23

Y
year 17
yellow 9
you'll 27

Appendix C: Words Taught in Level Three